More Praise for
My Dad, Yogi

"*My Dad, Yogi* is a beautifully depicted love story between Father and Son. Dale shares funny and unique reflections of what it was like growing up in the shadow of one of the most recognizable and beloved public figures of all time. I had such great respect for Yogi as a New York Yankee. I had tremendous adoration for Yogi as a Man. Dale captures the essence of both in this book."

—Joe Torre

"Baseball is a game that fathers teach their sons how to play. Life lessons are a lot tougher, for that's where they have to both learn from each other. Dale Berra's honest, humorous, and touching story is an intimate look at a relationship that was at times difficult, complicated, and tense, but true to who Yogi Berra was…always loving."

—Billy Crystal

"Touching on everything from Yogi's career and personal life to his relationship with Dale, *My Dad, Yogi* gives an intimate look at the life of an American icon."

—AskMen.com, Best Books for Father's Day

"A short, winsome memoir and biography of a winning American icon."

—*Library Journal*

"Just in time for Father's Day, *My Dad, Yogi*...is an entertaining and often moving story of a baseball family whose patriarch is perhaps the most quoted athlete in sports history."

—BookReporter.com

"Candid...a loving reflection on his famous father's achievements as baseball legend and family man."

—*New Jersey Monthly*

My Dad, Yogi

My Dad, Yogi

A Memoir of Family and Baseball

DALE BERRA

with Mark Ribowsky

hachette
BOOKS

NEW YORK   BOSTON

Hachette Books
Hachette Book Group
1290 Avenue of the Americas
New York, NY 10104
HachetteBooks.com
Twitter.com/HachetteBooks
Instagram.com/HachetteBooks

First Trade Paperback Edition: May 2020

Published by Hachette Books, an imprint of Perseus Books, LLC, a
subsidiary of Hachette Book Group, Inc. The Hachette Books name and
logo is a trademark of the Hachette Book Group.

The Hachette Speakers Bureau provides a wide range of authors for
speaking events. To find out more, go to www.hachettespeakersbureau.com
or call (866) 376-6591.

The publisher is not responsible for websites (or their content) that are not
owned by the publisher.

Library of Congress Control Number: 2018953672

ISBNs: 978-0-316-52545-9 (hardcover), 978-0-316-52544-2 (trade paperback),
978-0-316-52546-6 (ebook)

Printed in the United States of America

LSC-C

10 9 8 7 6 5 4 3 2 1

CONTENTS

INTRODUCTION

B-E-R-R-A

FIRST THINGS FIRST. Why did I write this book? The short answer is that I love my dad. That may sound obvious, but it is part of a larger answer: my dad's love for me did nothing less than save my life.

When he died in 2015 at a very well-lived ninety years of age, everyone knew Yogi Berra as an American icon, a legend of almost mythical proportions. Far fewer know me as the son who made it to the big leagues, following in his footsteps. I made it through ten years. I was on a world championship team, the '79 "We Are Family" Pittsburgh Pirates. I even set a record—not anything like my dad's stockpile of them but a rec-ord nonetheless—reaching first base seven times on catcher's interference. Hey, any way you can get on base, right? I'm sure Dad would have said just that. I once led baseball in hits by an eighth-place hitter in the lineup. I also played for my dad when he managed—for sixteen games—the '85 Yankees, the biggest thrill of my life, making me the first son to play for his father since Earle Mack on Connie Mack's Philadelphia Athletics in 1937. That's my piece of history.

I wasn't a great player, certainly not in the same universe as Dad. People in the stands would sometimes yell at me, "You'll never be as good as your old man!" But I always thought, who was? And I was fine with that.

I wasn't bad. I played third base and shortstop. Like Dad, I had a good glove. The bat? Not as much. I hit .238, had forty-nine home runs, 278 RBIs. I played in more games than any son of a Hall of Famer, 853, fifty-four more than Dick Sisler, son of George, and when I retired my dad and I had hit the most home runs by a father and son, 407 (since surpassed by the Fielders, Griffeys, and Bondses). Sure, I had only forty-nine, so that's like Tommie Aaron being able to say he and his brother hit more home runs than any brothers in history—with Tommie hitting only 742 fewer than Hank. But, hey, don't take that away from us.

The historians, the SABR crowd, rank me on the same level as players like Clete Boyer and Félix Mantilla. I'll take that. The flip side is, I had a chance to be better, much better, a star. When I came to the majors, I was only twenty and the best prospect in the minors. And while I don't make excuses for not being what I could have been, there's no doubt that my downfall was getting involved in the drug plague within the game during the '80s. Cocaine was the villain. It took my career away. I'm not alone. Ask Darryl Strawberry and Dwight Gooden. And Steve Howe. The Yankees, for some reason, have had a bunch of 'em.

Of course, I put more than a baseball career in jeopardy. And at the heart of this story is that it was my father and my family that turned me around. Only by hitting bottom did I learn what my dad had tried to teach me when I was a child growing up in his massive shadow. Those lessons are what I wanted to write about. I only wish I would have appreciated them when they could have saved my career.

I had a box-seat view of my father's life and death no one outside our family did, an intensely personal view of years that were both wonderful and painful for both of us. It's not every day that someone who's been written about as much as my father—and he was one of the most written about athletes of all time—can be seen in a new light. But I had that light, and after a great deal of soul-searching, I wanted to share it, because it was good for my soul. They call that a catharsis.

The other works about Dad were perfectly justified. A family friend of ours who helped establish the Yogi Berra Museum and Learning Center wrote a couple with Dad. His famous "Yogi-isms"—those observational baubles of fractured but solid logic—alone have filled more than a few books. People still haven't gotten their fill of him, because he was truly one of a kind as an American icon, a national treasure, and the most quoted man in the world. It's automatic that when his name is mentioned, people will reflexively smile. And yet no book has told of the Yogi I knew, the father of three sons, grandfather of eleven, great-grandfather of one. That is the story of us, our family, and it's one that only my brothers and I know.

In many ways, Dad and I both had to grow up and learn from each other what life really meant. I hope that when he died, he knew I loved him and had learned from him, that I carried his good name. And I hope I taught him that life has its pitfalls and we all arrive at our destination on different roads but end up on the same ground.

I don't think of this book as another Yogi history, but rather as a letter to him from my heart. That Dad was a legend is incidental to his role as a father needing to set his son straight. I knew that reliving the details of the story would be painful. It was something like therapy revealing a very stupid span of my life that reflected badly on him and wrecked a burgeoning career. Getting my two older brothers, Larry and Tim, and my oldest daughter, Whitney, to pitch in with their observations helped a lot, because their memories filled in gaps and allowed Yogi's boys to tell the story from all of our points of view.

I won't say it ain't easy being me, because I have been extremely fortunate to have grown up with the family I had and to have walked in the footsteps of my dad all the way into the big leagues. Yet I have to live with the shame and guilt of my descent. Today, three decades after I hung 'em up, I will walk through an airport or mall and someone will know me, even without the bushy, porn-movie mustache that was my signature as a player but I said goodbye to in the '90s. Maybe it's because, as I age, I look more like my dad. I've been told I look like I could still play. But my nose keeps getting bigger, my ears stick out more, and where's my hair going? Back in '75 when I was a nineteen-year-old wunderkind, my manager with the Pirates, Chuck Tanner, said I was "handsomer" than my father. I wish Chuck were still around, so he could say it again.

It's flattering, but only until someone will segue from "Hey, didn't you used to be...?" to "You had a drug problem, right?"

I can accept that. Because it's true. I used cocaine for over a decade. Richard Pryor once said he used Peru. Well, I used it through my promising career with the Pittsburgh Pirates, when I got swept up with ten other big-league players in the bust and trial of a Pittsburgh drug dealer in '85, baseball's second-biggest scandal since the "Black Sox" threw the 1919 World Series. You'd think that would have set me straight, but I kept using, thinking I had it all under control. Even after I retired and was arrested in a 1989 New Jersey drug investiga-tion, I had rationalizations, telling myself I was doing cocaine the "right" way, somehow within the rules.

I couldn't see how it had affected me and a career that went downhill. When the Pirates won it all in '79, Chuck said that my play late in the season filling in for our injured shortstop "won the pennant for us." Not Willie Stargell. Not Dave Parker. He also said I was half of the best shortstop–second base com-bination in the game, a future star. I didn't even know that I was throwing that future away. I could never foresee that, long into the future, an online writer would say that my rookie base-ball card "is a reminder that Dale Berra was once a poster child for cocaine running amok in pro sports."

These are all facts. I can't run away from them, because they cost me a major league career and a marriage, although I can add there was a happy ending, thanks to Dad and the tough-love support of my family. I got myself straight in time for him to be proud of me, after all. What I can't accept is that some people will blithely assume that my dad was to blame for his son's stupidity. He wasn't. Full stop. The poor choices I made, the delusions I lived with, didn't stem either consciously or sub-consciously from a bad childhood or resentment about living in his shadow. Those expecting a poison-pen, "Daddy Dearest"–type memoir can close the cover right now and stop reading. The truth is, I was walking in the footsteps of a giant shadow, but never did I feel it or any pressure to excel because I had the name B-E-R-R-A stitched across my back. I was on my own to sink or swim. We both wanted that.

But hands-off doesn't mean indifferent. He was always there for me, in his understated but unmistakably caring way. And he could only take so much of my self-destruction, not because his name was being soiled but because he hurt for me, seeing his flesh and blood ruining his life. He knew I knew better. In a way, the changing culture was to blame. Dad came from an era when players killed themselves with booze. He had watched Mickey Mantle do that in their glory days, like all the Yankees and the writers who covered them keeping it a secret from the public. But he himself never was a drunk; he knew his limits. And drugs were something he knew almost nothing about. When he managed the New York Mets in the '70s, half his team were regular potheads and he never even knew it. What I did was far worse.

And yet, generational differences aside, we were both Berras, descendants of Italian immigrants with a ferocious competitive instinct. Was he the perfect father? Who is? While he had that big, ingratiating smile, he wasn't an overly warm man. To us, he was strict but fair; just like the public Yogi, he didn't say much, but you knew where he stood. He was tough but forgiving. He didn't tell us he loved us—those words were reserved for

Mom—but we felt it. He had his rules we had to decipher and apply to our lives. My brothers did that better than I did, but, as crazy as it sounds, even when I was doing drugs those rules kept me from making it worse. I only hope he knew that in his soul.

He was good to people because he didn't have to think about being good. He just was. He was the most humble man who's ever lived, a guy who said so much by saying so little, even if the rest of the world did a double take when he uttered a Yogi-ism. They're so well known now that people know them by heart: "Baseball is 90 percent mental. The other half is physical." "You can observe a lot by watching." "It's déjà vu all over again." "You better cut the pizza in four pieces because I'm not hungry enough to eat six." "Never answer an anonymous letter." Even a president repeated one of them. In 2015, Dad was post-humously awarded the Presidential Medal of Freedom. President Barack Obama called him an extraordinary man, then, with a grin, "One thing we know for sure: if you can't imitate him, don't copy him."

I certainly never could have copied him. You can't success-fully copy an original. He is not an easy man to describe; he was neither as simple nor as complicated as people would alter-nately define him, because he could be both, in the space of a few seconds. Under his lovable facade there were real feel-ings and pain. He had to bury both of his parents within two years as a still-young man, and his fifteen-year exile from the Yankees after being fired in 1986 by George Steinbrenner after only sixteen games ate him up inside with anger very much unlike him. Ending that exile not only made the whole world feel better; it made *him* feel better. I had a lot to do with that, and I considered it repaying what he'd done for me.

All I could do was try to see life as he did, something I'm still trying to get right. That's why I call this a book about life; rather than being about my dad or me, it is about *us*, about our family, keeping the bonds between us strong, no matter what. It is a view of Yogi Berra seen only by his family, a view of a man larger than life who himself had to learn late in the game that life is not a fable after all, that there were lessons he had to learn from his son's failings so that they could be turned into success.

That was my saving grace. He is the reason I have not touched a drop of cocaine in twenty-seven years, nor substituted booze for it. I've stayed clean and sober, and I have never felt better than I do right now. I lost one family through no fault of theirs, but I remarried and became the father of two more beautiful daughters. And I could share the last years of Dad's life as the son he wanted. Rather than another well-worn, from-the-depths "drug" story, then, between these covers is a memoir of Yogi Berra from the point of view of his own flesh and blood, the son who could have been his legatee in baseball but found his real success being his legatee in life. Long after I stopped wearing a uniform, I feel B-E-R-R-A across my back and all the way to my soul. And I wear it with pride and joy.

CHAPTER 1

The Redoubtable Mr. Berra

LAWRENCE PETER BERRA—"the redoubtable Mr. Berra," as the great Red Barber used to call him during New York Yankee broadcasts back in the early '60s, or just "Mr. Berra" as Casey Stengel did—was a product of his environment, as was I. The difference was, he transcended poverty growing up in Dago Hill in St. Louis and pushed himself to an incredible level, to where real life read like fiction, as a miniature, ethnic version of a John Wayne character. He became ingrained in the fabric of the Greatest Generation that won the Big War and refused to accept defeat. At eighteen he was in a gunboat on D-Day, dodging German machine-gun fire. Any of a thousand images of him, his cap turned backward, shin guards and chest protector caked with dirt and sweat, pancake mitt ready to swallow up a pitch or a pop fly, is a picture of courage and character.

The familiar freeze-frames of his career are unforgettable, like him leaping like an overjoyed kid into Don Larsen's arms when the last out was made in Larsen's perfect World Series game against the Dodgers in 1956. Or drifting back when Bill

Mazeroski hit the first pitch in the bottom of the ninth in the 1960 Series. Dad always said he believed he would catch that game-winning homer. And if you look closely at the old films, the ball seemed to hang right over his head for a split second, as if he was willing it down to him. If it had dropped, nobody would have been surprised.

He had all the credentials a player could have: three-time MVP, eighteen-time All-Star, thirteen-time world champion. He was a fixture of sports' greatest dynasty, but also a player, coach, or manager on every single pennant-winning New York baseball team from 1947 to 1981. For many, he *was* baseball in New York. Yet he was also a symbol of something bigger than baseball. Because of his roots and coming into prominence when there was still anti-Italian discrimination, when he was honored by friends and businessmen on Dago Hill in 1951, someone said he was "one of the three best-known Italians in the world—Columbus, Marconi, and Yogi Berra." Not Joe DiMaggio, one of the greatest ballplayers of all time, but the squat little guy who looked like a Smurf. No one who ever saw him forgot him. Which is why, in 2017, one sports columnist asked: "How About Yogi Berra Day—Why Columbus?"

I regret to say I never saw him play in person. In fact, I never rooted for his team until it was no longer the Yankees but the crosstown Mets when he managed them in the early 1970s. But I was there for Larsen's perfect game—in my mom's stomach. She was eight months pregnant as she sat in the stands that day with Merlyn Mantle and Joan Ford, Whitey's wife, watching each out, the last coming when a pinch hitter, a utility player named Dale Mitchell, was called out on a half-swing for strike three. Mom told Joan that if Mitchell made the last out, she was going to name the baby Dale. She liked the sound of it and that it could be given to a boy or a girl.

Dad, of course, went along. He was friends with everybody in baseball, but I'm sure he didn't have any special relationship with Dale Mitchell. Still, I have a sneaking suspicion it meant something to him, because of how his mind worked. He might have wanted to make the moment live through his son. At least that's my theory; Dad would never have thought too deeply about it. He just did things and they usually worked out fine. As that name has for me.

During his Hall of Fame career, he wasn't Yogi to me. That was more like a public thing, a brand name, one perfect for him. He'd worn it since he was a kid, meaning that even back then he was a wise man, not a wise guy. Even Mom called him Yogi, but to his sons he was Dad, the guy who came home after Sunday home games and sat at the head of the table, tearing into the veal parmigiana. He always had to sit at the head of the table and have both ends of the Italian bread. No one could touch a heel of that bread but Dad.

There was no ESPN back then, no MLB Network, no internet to endlessly watch highlights on. Baseball—all sports, really—lived through box scores and game stories in the newspapers. I was too young to read them. I was watching cartoons—one of them being Yogi Bear, who also played in a big park, Jellystone. I had no idea that Yogi was named after Dad, though the producers, Hanna-Barbera, who created so many cartoons in TV's early days, ludicrously said it was just a coincidence. Dad even sued them for defamation. It wasn't that he couldn't take a joke, but when someone uses your name for a cartoon character and doesn't even ask for permission, much less pay you a dime, you don't accept that. Dad may have looked funny, but he was nobody's fool, on or off the diamond. But Dad didn't object because he was owed money; it was because he was owed respect.

He did eventually drop the suit, because technically his name was Larry, not Yogi, so it complicated an open-and-shut case. He just shrugged and let it go, like all the other jokes about him, and took it as flattery, although he never knew why he wasn't being paid for it. The joke never died, even when he did. When the AP wire service first reported on his death, it wrote: "New York Yankees Hall of Fame catcher Yogi Bear has died. He was 90." In truth, Yogi Bear lives on, sort of like Dad, in suspended animation.

He did more TV appearances than most players. The only times that kids saw the faces of their favorite ballplayers was on the Game of the Week or local telecasts, or the old *Home Run Derby* TV show. Dad never made it onto that show, not being a big home run hitter. That was for the matinee-idol long-ball guys, Mantle, Mays, Aaron, Killebrew. But Madison Avenue loved Dad during the first decade of the new invention called television. A team that won like clockwork, with about as much flair and exertion, whose big star was a blond god with a Li'l Abner physique and the too-good-to-be-true name Mickey Mantle, had seemed exempt from the truism of Yankee haters that "rooting for the Yankees is like rooting for U.S. Steel." As Mickey once said, "He was the guy who made the Yankees seem almost human."

That must have been why I saw flickering images of him on our TV, in commercials, smoking a cigarette, selling a car, whatever else someone would pay him a few bucks to say he used. I can all too clearly remember the commercials he did for Yoo-Hoo—the chocolate drink's sales skyrocketing when it became synonymous with Yogi—with the punchline "It's Me-He for Yoo-Hoo!" (Another Yogi-ism happened when he was asked if Yoo-Hoo was hyphenated; he replied, "It ain't even carbonated.") He also did a cameo on the *Phil Silvers Show*, with Mickey, Whitey Ford, Phil Rizzuto, and Gil McDougald. They played themselves posing as Southern squires, helping Sergeant Bilko convince a phenom pitcher who was a Southern boy, played by Dick Van Dyke, to sign with the Yankees. The highlight was Dad, wearing a cutaway morning coat, stealing the scene by saying in his best Bronx drawl, "Arrivederci, y'all!"

Another appearance was in 1964 when he was the mystery guest on *What's My Line?*, signing in to thunderous applause, his championship pinkie ring glistening, and then squeaking a high-pitched "yes" or "no" to the panel's questions—the voice he often used to disguise himself when he picked up the telephone, in case it was someone he didn't want to talk to. They got who he was very quickly, the actress Arlene Francis asking, "Are you the Yankee doodle dandy, Yogi Berra?" Mom even got to come out and take a bow. The funniest moment was when one of the panelists asked, "Do you work for a non-profit-making organization?" That broke him up but good. Almost as funny was when another asked, "What if you woke up tomorrow morning and found out you were the manager of the Mets?" His answer, "Well, I don't know yet." Maybe he knew something.

Those Yankee stars were celebrities—the very first mystery guest on *What's My Line?* was Scooter Rizzuto. A Yankee sighting was a big deal. Mom and Dad were sitting in the first row when Marciano knocked out Joe Louis at Yankee Stadium in September 1950. Joe fell through the ropes and almost landed into Dad's lap. And sitting right behind them was Boris Karloff, who played Frankenstein and was great friends with them. Movie stars would be thrilled seeing *them*. The big in-spot for stars of all kinds was Toots Shor's Restaurant on Broadway. You'd look around the dining room and see Jackie Gleason and Frank Sinatra mingling with Joe DiMaggio. Dad liked it because Toots always protected you from the other patrons. That's why he went there, not to be seen but to be with people he admired and because Mom liked to mingle more than he did. Before the night was over, the movie stars would be at their table, schmoozing.

Joe D loved Dad during the brief time their careers intersected—back in those pre–politically correct times, the Yankees dubbed them "Big Dago and Little Dago." Joe always had an entourage, the first athlete to have one. He got picked up at airports and train terminals, never rode the team bus, always had people waiting for him, never stayed at the team hotel but in luxury in people's homes. That was class. The players never saw him outside the park. And if you were a Berra or Rizzuto and he said, "Come out to dinner with me," you had to go, and you had to be dressed properly. You couldn't say no. One time, he invited Mom and Dad out to meet Marilyn Monroe and go to dinner. Joe was very guarded, and he would never introduce anyone to Marilyn. He kept her almost like a prisoner. But he thought enough of Mom and Dad to have them meet her. Dad said he could think of only one thing to say when he met her—*marone*.

There was also the time Frank was playing at a club in town, and my brother Larry, who's a huge fan, wanted to go see him. The show was sold out, so Dad said, "I'll call Frank." Just like that. He never said he knew him, but he could just reach into his little black book and ring him up. *That's* what being a Yankee, and being Yogi Berra, meant.

My first decade of life coincided with the last hurrah of the Yankee dynasty, which began after Dad came up in 1947 and they won five straight American League pennants from 1949 to 1953, four more from '55 to '58, then another five from '60 to '64, the last of them when Dad was their manager. I watched the later World Series on the tube and was beginning to know him as more than just Dad, although he never once acted like a star or boasted about himself. Baseball was his job. His life was as a husband and father.

When he began taking me out to Yankee Stadium, as early as the late '50s when I was still a toddler, I was more taken with the pageantry of it, the brilliant green and brown field, how the baby blue seats rose forever into the blue sky, above the unforgettable picket fence–like frieze facade lining the roof of the enormous upper deck. There was even a photo in the *Daily News* after the last game of the '59 season of Dad in the locker room carrying two duffel bags, with, as the caption read,

"Little Dale Berra, 2, help[ing] his famous dad, Yogi, carry a bat from Yankee Stadium." Carry? That bat looked so big on my shoulder, it seemed to be carrying *me*. (I was also blond then. That didn't last long.)

I got attention for being the little tyke Yogi would sometimes hold in his massive arms. I also remember that Mickey would squirt me with the hose from the whirlpool. I'd walk past him, and he'd let me have it. He'd get Dad, too, all the time. He'd whisper to me, "Kid, watch your dad. I put some Ben-Gay in his hat. His head's gonna start itching in a second." And sure enough, Dad would start furiously scratching his noggin. I admit, it was pretty funny. I didn't tell Dad, but he knew, and he didn't mind being the butt of Mickey's jokes because it kept those guys loose. Also, Mickey could crush an anvil in his hands.

There were times when his Yankee buddies would come to our house across the George Washington Bridge in Montclair, New Jersey. Everyone loved him and Mom; it was a real extended family, unlike the individualistic vibe of team sports today. Dad and Mickey would sit in the den drinking vodka and bullshitting. Away from the sportswriters, he was loud and unrestrained with his teammates, not with Yogi-isms but jokes and stories that had Mickey on the floor. Believe me, he could talk all day if he wanted. With his sons, though, he wasn't there to entertain or unwind; he was there to raise us right.

When Mickey would bring his two sons, Mickey Jr. and Dave, with him, Larry, Timmy, and I would take them into the backyard to play wiffleball, and we would kick their asses every game. We had Dad's ferocious competitive streak. We had to win. Dad taught me that, but he never really taught me the game or how to play it. "That's what your brothers are for," he'd say. It wasn't that he was ignoring me. It was just that there was a chain of command among his boys.

When Larry was born in 1949, I think Dad may have been more hands-on about showing him how to play, but when Tim, who came along in 1951, and I arrived, Dad had nothing to do with it. I really learned all I had to on my own. All three of us were lucky enough to have his genes, the ones that blessed us with athletic talent and coordination. But that was all Dad handed down. Everything else, we had to find out by ourselves, or get from Mom.

TIM BERRA: He wasn't what you would call a warm, affectionate man. And I think all of us kids have gotten that trait from him, unfortunately. I wish I could say there were moments when he got sentimental, like at confirmations, graduations, weddings, funerals, but I never saw a tear running down his face. Mom was the emotional, touchy-feely one. Dad was supportive, he was always there, he came to as many of our school games as he could, but didn't fawn over us. Even when he took us to the stadium, and he did that quite a bit when we were little kids, it would be Mickey who would hit me balls, play catch with me, not Dad.

That's how he was, but Dad was also a very smart man. He knew the complications of raising three sons who might want to play sports, and he had it all thought out; his distance was meant to let us flourish on our own. Would I say he was a good father? No. He was a great father.

LARRY BERRA: Actually, Dale is wrong about Dad teaching me. He didn't consider that to be his role as a father. That was his business. But here's the kind of father he was. Mom told me once, "You and your brothers would never have to work a day in your life if your father wanted to travel in the winter time." Because after the season was over, he had many offers, to open stores, do ribbon-cuttings, make appearances. In the '50s, Hertz was just starting and opened rental car franchises all over the country. They wanted him to go all over for them, but he turned them down to stay home.

Not that he was sacrificing much. He and Mickey were in incredible demand locally, from Yankee sponsors. He'd do Ballantine beer, Brylcreem, Marlboro cigarettes, Gillette razors. Someone would hand him a hundred-dollar bill and take his picture with the product. You'd see his face everywhere in magazines, newspapers, local TV. When Yoo-Hoo came along, it was a Jersey-based company, so he did their commercials because one of his best friend's fathers invented the drink. My perk was that I could drive my car down to the factory and fill my trunk up with Yoo-Hoo. I'd tell people, "Hey, I got Yoo-Hoo." I made a lot of friends that way.

I never doubted that Dad was a caring father. He would take us with him to play golf at a country club, travel to see the relatives in St. Louis. When I was nine, ten, eleven, Dad even took me on Yankee road trips. I went on the train with him, which was how they traveled then. I went to Boston and Baltimore, and they were all so close. Even now. I just got back from playing in a softball tournament in Myrtle Beach, South Carolina, and I called up Bobby Richardson, who lives there, just to see how he's doing. And he actually came over and watched us play. Those guys were like my family. It's not like that in the game anymore.

Timmy and I were luckier than Dale. They still played mainly day games when we were young, so Dad would be back for dinner almost every night. When Dale got older, they were playing all night games and he'd be asleep when Dad got home and at school before he woke up. But during the winter, when Dale had hockey practice, Dad would be up at four a.m., because practice would be at five. He'd open Dale's door and say, "Come on, kid, rise and shine."

When I was thirteen, I went on my first road trip with Dad, with the Mets to Montreal and Chicago. He took me to the movies in Montreal. I remember we saw *Beneath the Planet of the Apes* and loved it. That was 1970, the year after the Mets' amazin' championship, and Dad and I felt on top of the world. For him, all that travel was commonplace. He'd logged more miles than an old Dodge. For me, it was a whole new world. It was like I was hanging with some of the most famous athletes in sports, flying on the team plane—a United 5000 charter, the one the Mets used all the time. I was a mini celebrity, I suppose. The pilots let me sit in a jump seat in the cockpit during takeoffs and landings.

It was early, but it was obvious this was the life I wanted to live, this was my future. How could I not want it to be? I stayed at luxury hotels with the champion New York Mets, came to the park with them on the team bus, put on a uniform and took fly balls hit by Cleon Jones and Tommie Agee, fielded grounders with Buddy Harrelson. I'd take batting practice. I could find a light bat, one that a pitcher used, and even at a young age I could make people sit up and take notice, because I was a natural hitter. Dad would also arrange for me to work as a visiting bat boy, at Wrigley Field—how's that for a memory?

The next year, he took me on the Mets' West Coast swing, to LA, San Francisco, and San Diego, where we went to the San Diego Zoo. We would spend all day together before we went to the ballpark. He always had plans for me. We did everything together, and it was very bonding, the kind of father-son relationship most kids can only dream of. But Dad was more than a sports legend. He was the man who brought me up, and those times with him on the road were really the first times in my life that I got to spend alone with Dad, just me and him, away from everybody. He may not have been a man who said a whole lot, but he really took care of me; that was as important to him as preparing for a game. And those are memories that will last a lifetime.

My brothers and I were so lucky that we had two amazing parents who would have done anything for their kids. Yogi's better half wasn't only a great mom; she was a smart, classy, caring woman. The world knew Carmen Berra almost as much as they knew her husband the legendary Yankee. She could certainly make both men and women do a double take. Actually, both of them could, especially when they were out together.

They were like a royal couple. And Mom, a beautiful, striking blonde, with an amazing sense of style.

There is a photograph of Mom in 1968 taken during a fashion show put on by wives of ballplayers. Wearing a black sleeveless dress with a big buckle on the waist, she could have been a fashion model, her body language graceful and poised, walking by spectators and other wives, some of whom seemed transfixed, almost with their jaws hanging open. They say opposites attract, and sometimes they do in storybook ways. Mom was the beauty who somehow married the beast.

When they would go out on the town, she looked like a movie star, and because of her, so did he. If we have good looks, she gave them to us. That's not being mean to Dad; it's just a fact. He said the same thing, and could laugh about it because it was he, the beast, who got the beauty. To the day she died, he looked at her like a lovesick teenager. I don't think he ever quite believed she had fallen in love with him. Dad had that cuddly, teddy-bear quality, but he knew he had married up, way up.

Unlike her operatic namesake, Carmen Short Berra was no gypsy. Dad's ancestors came over on a boat from Italy. Mom's came over on the *Mayflower*. Okay, I'm exaggerating. It just seemed that way because of how classy she was. But when they met back in their hometown St. Louis, her family had been entrenched for decades in a rural farming town called Howes Mill, Missouri, where she grew up with no plumbing or electricity and an outhouse in the back for a good portion of her youth. Her family always reminded me of the sisters in *Petticoat Junction*. Dad's brothers were Uncle Tony and Uncle Mike. Her sisters were Marylou, Nadine, Bonnie May, and Donna.

Talk about your all-American, county fair, farmers' daughters. Her cousins we'd call Uncle Claude and Aunt Ismus. (Nadine also married an Italian boy, named Palermo.) They were typical Midwest Baptists, very Bible Belt. My grandfather Ernest Short read the Bible to Mom and her sisters and brother every night.

Not to name-drop, but Robert E. Lee may be in our family tree. No bull. Mom's middle name was Lee, and she insisted it was after the Confederate general, who was somewhere in her mother's family tree. I don't know, since General Lee was from Virginia. But Mom said somewhere in their ancestry they were related. If I was handed down the leadership qualities of Yogi Berra and Robert E. Lee, I'll take it.

When they met over the winter of '48. Dad was still living in St. Louis in the off-season, and she was a waitress in a restaurant called Biggie's. As in *The Godfather*, when he saw her he was hit by the thunderbolt. In Dad's words, she was a "knockout," the highest praise a man could give a girl back then. Shy as he was, he summoned up all his nerve, marched right up to her, and asked for a date. Mom was only the third girl he ever dated, but he knew she was the one, even if she wasn't Italian, which meant he'd have to convince Grandpa Pietro and Grandma Paolina that she was worthy of *him*. But he didn't need to convince Mom. She fell for him right away; to her, the guy some called an ogre was actually strong, masculine—yes, even sexy. That summer, she helped stuff the ballot boxes to get him chosen for the All-Star Game, and he was, the first of his eighteen selections, still third in the American League after Mickey's twenty and Cal Ripken's nineteen.

Dad had it made with her, but he got the lesson of his life when he pulled back. Thinking his career was too important for love, he stood Mom up on a date, knowing she would be mad as hell because he didn't even call her, just didn't show up, and it embarrassed her with her friends. Mom really let him have it. She told him she had a lot of guys just dying to date her, which was absolutely true. She did some reverse psychology on him, adding in that she had a good job waitressing, making $90 a week, and maybe she wasn't ready to settle down herself. Well, that did the trick. For a while, Dad was so ashamed that he stopped coming down to Biggie's, for fear he would run into her. And Biggie told Dad he wanted him to be there, it helped business, and he liked Dad so much. He said, "Yogi, get her back." And Dad always knew good advice when he heard it. He knew he'd made a big mistake and came crawling back. She forgave him. He asked her to have dinner with him and the whole family. When she was looking away, he dropped a ring on her plate. When she saw it, she was stunned silent, but nodded yes. They tied the knot on January 26, 1949, at St. Ambrose Church. By then, Mom had converted to Catholicism out of love for Dad, and she also loved the trappings of the Catholic Church.

He certainly showed he would do anything for her; on that blessed day, he wore a tuxedo for the first time in his life, and even a white carnation on his lapel. She, of course, looked resplendent in her long gown and tiara. And from that day on, she also wore the pants. Mom was really the rock of the family. Dad was away for long periods of time on road trips and two months for spring training, so she was both mother and father.

But even when he was home, she was the one who woke us up and got us on the school bus, and she'd be waiting when we got home. She was the one who sent us to our rooms when we misbehaved. She was the hands-on parent, and Larry, Timmy, and I are as much a product of her as we are of Dad. He gave us the stuff of our dreams, but she was the one who made sure we believed we could achieve them.

Mom was a real intellectual; she read tons of books. Mom gave deep thought to everything. She was a rock-ribbed Republican. Her brother, Norman, was an NRA member. And she admired William F. Buckley for his erudite manner. Dad would go along with her opinion of things. Like most immigrants, his family worshiped Franklin D. Roosevelt. The Berras were working-class men, union men. But he voted for Republicans because Mom said so. No kitchen-table debates were necessary.

That's not to say he didn't have opinions of his own, but he wouldn't pretend that he wasn't an eighth-grade dropout. As a teenager during the Depression, he had to work so his family could eat. And he saw his baseball career pretty much the same way. He wasn't playing for ego; even as a living legend, he was playing so we had food on the table.

LARRY: She was a registered Republican, but she voted for the person who she thought was best for the position. She formed quick opinions of people. If she liked you,

you got the vote. And Dad hated labels but, more than that, phonies. He wouldn't say much about issues, but he watched the news, and if someone was a phony, he'd grunt derisively. I guess that's why he wouldn't come out for candidates. They all wanted that, but it was just for his name, his popularity. Mom and I would watch debates on TV, and he'd go upstairs and put on a sitcom. Mom would have had a field day with this Trump stuff, trying to make sense of it all. I can hear her saying, "This is crazy, I've never seen anything like this." And I can just see Dad, who saw the country survive the Depression and about six wars, shaking his head, laughing and saying, "Wait 'til tomorrow, it'll get crazier."

People have asked me if Dad's public persona was a put-on, as if he played a lovable, somewhat befuddled character someone later called the "Yoda of the Yankees," then came home and was a loudmouthed tyrant or something. I can honestly say he was the same exact person at home. And, yes, there were the same kind of say-what Yogi-isms, which I wish I could remember in full but don't because they just rolled out of his mouth so naturally. My brothers and I and Mom would tell him, "You just said another one." Mom would tell him if it was funny or not. If it was, she would write it down, like a stenographer, for future use. Because he wouldn't remember them right after he said them.

He'd be asked about something, such as meeting the pope,

and say, "He must read the papers a lot, because he said, 'Hello, Yogi.' And I said, 'Hello, Pope.'" Or seeing Steve McQueen in a movie and saying, "He must have made that before he died." Or the one about him observing, after being told a Jewish lord mayor had been elected in Dublin, "Only in America can a thing like this happen."

Actually, only in America could a Yogi Berra have happened. I find it hilarious that books have been written by very smart people analyzing those sayings as "pop philosophy." One of those smart people, Roy Blount Jr., remarked that they were "less in the tradition of the *Bhagavad-Gita* than in that of Mark Twain, who observed that the music of Richard Wagner was 'better than it sounds.'" Some call them malapropisms, contradictions, roundabout veracity—or tautologies. Dad himself didn't know if he said everything he said—see how easy it is to do it? A lot of folks thought they were made up by Joe Garagiola, who grew up with Dad in St. Louis on the Hill and had a much better career telling Yogi stories on TV and at banquets than he had as a big-league catcher. Those stories helped make Joe famous and later in his life the lead baseball broadcaster for NBC and co-host of *Today*. Dad never claimed to be Aristotle or Plato. He just knew that whatever he said, he was a basic guy telling a basic truth from his, shall we say, unique perspective.

He provided fodder for others to use as comic material, not just Joe, but Jimmy Piersall, the Cleveland Indians outfielder who recovered from a mental breakdown and became a great storyteller, used to recall asking Dad, "Why don't you get your kids an encyclopedia?" The answer (according to Jimmy)?

"Listen here, buddy, when I went to school, I walked. So can they." Of course, nobody told the line better than Dad himself. He would get tons of invitations to speak at school graduations, business luncheons, whatever. And he had a set speech, where he would weave homespun motivation. Instead of lame clichés, he'd sit in his den and take time writing them out, not just a string of a bunch of known Yogi-isms, but new ones created for the occasion, making a point about life.

"How's this one sound?" he'd ask, then read: "If the world was perfect, it wouldn't be." Or: "Be careful if you don't know where you're going in life, because you might not get there." You couldn't help but see how savvy he was at self-parody to help get across his very sound advice. And even though he didn't really like attention, if there was one thing he loved after Mom and playing baseball, it was playing the role of Yogi Berra.

In reality, men of great intellect gravitated to him. Everyone familiar with Yogi lore knows the story of him rooming with Bobby Brown on the Yankees in the '50s. Bobby, who would become a doctor, would be in the room reading *Gray's Anatomy* while Dad read comic books—"How'd your story come out?" Dad supposedly asked. But let me tell you, there must have been something in those comic books nobody else saw. And Bobby didn't want to make conversation with anyone else, so draw your own conclusions about how much Dad meant to men with sharp minds. They envied him for being able to seem dumb while being so smart.

Really, he didn't say much, which was why the Yogi-isms

stood out. During one of Dad's managerial stints, his great buddy Phil Rizzuto said, "Yogi gives short answers. And they're all mixed in with grunts. But that doesn't mean he doesn't know as much as managers who'll talk forever." Remember, he was a child of the '30s, a product of the '40s, a household name in the '50s. Those were decades when stern, stoic, hardworking fathers ruled the home. But the children of those fathers loved them and knew when they got their point across. The memories of him that are etched in my mind are of the long, endless hours spent together on road trips, but I don't know that I ever spoke with him in depth about school or even baseball. He just wasn't that kind of father.

Do I wish he had been more verbal, more expansive in his thoughts? Yes. We could have been less sheltered. Looking back, I would have liked it if he had taken me into his den, closed the door, and like Ward Cleaver related the perfect story about right and wrong, so Beaver would never do what he did again, at least until the next episode. I don't think Dad was capable of that. It wasn't innate to him. If it was, he wouldn't have been Yogi Berra.

We Baby Boomers like to say that the *Father Knows Best* portrait of America in the '50s really didn't exist. But it did exist. We had some scenes in our house like those on TV. Mom would come downstairs and tell us, "Look at your dad. Isn't he handsome?" She'd sit down and just smile at Dad. It was something from a Norman Rockwell painting. Dad was his own version of Ward. He was there for you; he just didn't have a long story to tell to make his point.

You wouldn't have thought he ever worried, ever doubted

himself. But he did. He once told a *Sports Illustrated* writer, "I worry about keeping Carm happy so she won't be sorry she married me, about the kids growing up good, and about keeping out of trouble with God. I worry a lot." In that article, he told of having trouble sleeping on the road, and that Phil Rizzuto read him bedtime stories to get him to doze off. Scooter recalled, "He said the sound of my voice put him to sleep. I often thought of that when I started broadcasting." The article also quoted Mom saying, "I don't know why people think he's so relaxed. He's a basket case!"

I never saw Dad like that, as anything other than a rock, because he never let me see anything else. I think I might have caught a glimpse if he'd ever given me "the talk," the one fathers are supposed to give their sons about sex but usually chicken out. Not that I needed that talk. This was the time of bra burning, free love, women's liberation, and X-rated movies. What was he gonna say that I didn't already know? But for something like that, he had his standard answer: "Ask your brothers." Then he probably said to himself, "Whew!"

LARRY: He only did "the talk" with me. I remember coming home when I was fifteen or sixteen, and Mom said, "Your father wants to talk to you." I said, "About what?" She said, "Just go up, it's time for your father to talk." And so I go up and he was in his room. He kind of smiled awkwardly and you knew he only agreed to do this because of Mom. His heart really wasn't in it, and he had no idea what to say. After a minute, he was ready.

"Eh, you already know everything you need to know about sex and all that kind of stuff. Good night."

And he was right, as always. We all knew about sex. That's why I never gave Timmy "the talk" and Timmy never gave it to Dale. Hell, I think Dad thought we might teach him a few things.

It had to be hard for him to come to grips with the '60s. The antiwar marches and draft-card burning, the assassinations, the confusion and cultural differences clashed with everything he and his generation knew. But even he got to the point where he didn't defend the war. "Let's get this thing over with and bring 'em home," he'd say. In his generation, stalemates and moral victories didn't count, only winning. But, as he also knew, you can't win 'em all.

True, he was in the middle of a lot of change. But he was never a get-off-my-lawn guy. He could understand that younger generations had their own lifestyles. That was why in the '80s players who could have been his children—and one who actually was his child—loved him. But if you would have told him he lived like it was still the '50s, he wouldn't have argued with you. Let's not forget that he once said, "The future ain't what it used to be." Just try to argue with that. Yet, within the game itself, he was a part of a different breed. Jumping into Larsen's arms, that was radical. Watching grainy baseball highlight movies, it always amazes me how little celebrating those guys did. Maybe there'd be a slap on the back, but no one lingered at the plate watching the home run rise or flipped the bat away with a flourish. The unwritten rule was that you didn't show up the other team. It was called sportsmanship. Well, there's never been a better sportsman than Yogi Berra. But he made it possible—or necessary, as he would say—to show your emotions when you win, even playing for U.S. Steel.

The Larsen leap wasn't the first such display of his, nor the last. When the last out of the '52 Series against the Dodgers was made, he raced out to Yankee relief pitcher Bob Kuzava and piggyback rode him. And let's not forget that unbelievable back-and-forth game 7 against the Pirates in 1960. When he came to bat in the top of the sixth, two men on, one out, trailing 4-2, he got hold of a 0-1 fastball from Roy Face, a fantastic reliever, and crushed it into the right field seats. Halfway down the first-base line, he shot his fist in the air and vaulted a foot off the ground. I think of that as the model for Carlton Fisk's "body English" homer in the '75 World Series. And no one on the Pirates thought he was showing them up. Because he never would have. (If only he could have jumped high enough to catch Mazeroski's homer.)

Not that he didn't have a ton of pride, in himself, his team, his league. Back then, your league was like your family, too. When the Yankees came back to win the '58 Series against the Milwaukee Braves, Dad smirked, "Those National League guys were getting pretty smart," meaning smart-assed, for their boasting early in the series.

He was stoic, contained, but full of fire inside. He didn't yell, didn't spank us. The only time he would show anger was if we were disrespectful to Mom. Then you got the hand, the back of his hand that wore a World Series ring—which he wore on his pinkie, which was as big as most people's ring finger. You could look in the mirror and see "5"—which was engraved on the ring, for the team's five straight championships—on your cheek. I'm not kidding. I'm only glad he wasn't wearing the Hickok Belt they give away to the athlete of the year. That would have been Mom's job. She used to use a belt, but just on the legs, completely nonabusive but the message was received.

LARRY: He only got mad at me and Timmy one time that I can remember. We lived at Woodcliff Lake, and Timmy and I flooded the bathroom. We plugged up the drain in the tub and it overflowed, and Dad really got mad. It's the only time he got us with the strap. And it was the last time. Because he could just look at you and you knew it was time to stop. The tough one was really my mother. She would pull your hair, pinch you, all kinds of stuff. She was the disciplinarian. Most of the time when we would ask Dad for something, he'd say, "Go ask your mother." She could be a softie, though. When I was fifteen or sixteen I wanted to take this girl to the movies. I asked my dad for five dollars and he said, "Go get a job." But Mom gave me the five dollars and said, "Don't tell your father." That was what Mama Paolina told Dad when he asked for money as a teenager. With us, the apples never fell far from the tree.

With both Mom and Dad, if you did something wrong you'd know about it, but in the end it would be "It's okay, don't worry about it, you're a good kid, you'll be all right." And you know what? That's exactly what Dad did when he managed. He never wanted to have anybody mad at him and never wanted to disappoint anybody. If he took a pitcher out, he'd feel bad about it.

After the game he would talk to the guy about why. He wouldn't say, "You gave up four straight hits, what the hell was wrong with you?" He would say, "I want you to know why I brought in the other guy," and explain that it was because of the percentages, which pitcher had better success against the next hitter. Because he knew all the numbers in his head. He had a computer in there.

Dad would analyze the game and the at-bats, in that internal computer, which also made him a brilliant poker and gin player. He wasn't a mathematician, but you threw out three or four cards playing gin and he'd tell you what you had in your hand. He was known as the best gin player in every country club he ever played in. Timmy played a lot of gin at the Montclair Golf Club with him. He'd tell me, "Dale, you can't believe it. Before guys know what they've got in their hands, Dad's shifting his hand around and ready to go. I don't know how he does that. He's a freaking machine."

Machine or not, he was one of a kind. A lot of the stars from that era, DiMaggio, Mickey, Billy Martin, had a little meanness to them, could be pricks at times. It was like a badge of manhood. Billy would say, "I took you out because you're horseshit." But Dad wanted to be liked. When he managed me on the Yankees, after one game he even knocked on Dave Righetti's door at the hotel to make sure Rags knew why he took him out. Dad didn't apologize, because he wasn't wrong. But while it sounds trite and corny, his players were like sons to him—which is why he *didn't* treat me like any more of a son than them. In Yogi world, you didn't get points for being anybody's son.

LARRY: That's true, but at some time or another people called all three of us "Yogi." When you met your friends, they'd go, "Hi, Yogi." I'm going to be sixty-nine, and I still play and manage in a competitive senior softball league. And the guys on my team, when someone asks who the manager is, they'll say, "Yogi, he's over there." We didn't want that; it just happened. When I was young, I cringed at it. Now, in my old age, I cherish it.

I never felt any pressure. I mean, who can possibly live up to a legend? You don't even try. And so I never felt that I was going to cash in on being Yogi's son, and few ever treated me like I was only that. I consciously didn't wear number 8. That was Dad's. It's retired at Yankee Stadium with all the other great Yankee numbers. I wasn't ever going to be an all-time great. In my heart, I was satisfied I gave all I had, that I was either good or bad on my own. Dad taught me that, and I listened.

I listened to everything he said. I even listened to the music he liked. Mom and Dad would put on Dean Martin, Buddy Greco, the Mills Brothers, the Andrews Sisters. Timmy, Larry, and I would love it. In the '70s, we'd go from Led Zeppelin to Duke Ellington, from "Stairway to Heaven" to "Satin Doll." It's not like we wanted to, but if Dad said, "You'll like this," we invariably found a reason to like it. And once in a while, he would sneak a listen to the rock-and-roll stations. That was a small victory.

Unlike most people, Dad only had one "enemy" in his life. That, of course, was George Steinbrenner, who broke a promise not to fire him. But even that feud was repaired. People always called Yogi Berra a player's manager, which means a manager players love and swear by. He won because his players would run through walls for him—almost literally, such as when Rusty Staub crashed into the right field wall at Shea Stadium in the '73 World Series, injuring his shoulder. Rusty courageously kept playing, virtually with one arm, just as Dad would have if he had to in his day. And don't think he couldn't be tough. He was. He wouldn't let any player disobey his rules, same as he wouldn't let his kids. Whatever it was, players responded to him.

The first two times he managed, he won the pennant right off the bat, both times coming from behind in August, with the '73 Mets from way behind. It was Tug McGraw who coined that team's creed—"Ya Gotta Believe!" But it was Dad—whose own version was the classic Yogi-ism "It ain't over 'til it's over"— who made them believe.

Absentee father? A noncaring father? Forget about it. As insular as he was, he always would make sure we would spend time together. My mind is filled with scattered moments of those times. Not just the road trips. Like when we sat in our den watching *Honeymooners* repeats, which were on all the time on New York TV. He'd be almost on the floor in laughter, which was something to see because it was infectious. Later, in the '70s, he saw the Dudley Moore comedy *Arthur* over and over. He said it was his favorite movie. Since it was about getting caught between the moon and New York City, I guess he could identify with it.

What I knew, but had to relearn, was that Dad had an innate instinct of what was right and wrong as well as one of the sharpest minds ever. The smartest Yogi-ism he ever said was "You can't hit and think at the same time," something I found out in my career. Boy, did I find out. I also found out the truth in a similar one: "Slump? I ain't in no slump. I just ain't hitting." Another Yogi-ism? Maybe. But for a man bred as a perfect baseball machine, without ever looking anything like one, these kinds of remarks were a looking glass into why he was. In the mind of Yogi Berra, if he was down, nothing on God's green earth was going to keep him down for long. And nothing did, until almost every organ in his body shut down. And it took ninety very full and wonderful years for that to happen.

CHAPTER 2

Number 8

MOST FANS KNOW the outline of Dad's life, which he would fill in for us from time to time. He was born Lorenzo Pietro Berra, though around Dago Hill in St. Louis the children of immigrants, as first-generation Americans, anglicized their names. Lorenzo Pietro Berra morphed into Lawrence Peter Berra—which, never legally changed, was on his contracts—and, to most who grew up with him, Larry, though his parents took to calling him "Lawdie" in their thick accents, unable to pronounce *Larry*. His driver's license read Lawrence Peter Berra—so, no, *Yogi* was never a legal or official name. Funny, though, how much pride those kids had when they spoke of Dago Hill. That was their pride and joy, their families, their friends. That was what tight-knit means.

His dad, Grandpa Pietro, came from Malvaglio, close to Milan, and Dad used to tell us how tough Pietro was. He had to be because the family had nothing. Pietro had come over in 1909 on the long boat ride from Italy, leaving his wife, Paolina, there until he could get settled, which he did in St. Louis, working in a brickyard. Dad used to tell me Grandpa had hands like a strop. He used to pick the bricks up in the brickyard bare-handed, and his forearms, hands, and fingers felt like an elephant's hide. If you ever crossed Pietro, he would whack you with the back of his hand, and it would feel like a sock filled with thumbtacks.

Pietro sent for Paolina in 1912, along with Uncle Tony and Uncle Mike, who joined them on the Hill and lived in a cramped house on Elizabeth Avenue. The family expanded again when a third son, John, was born in 1922 and then, on May 12, 1925, Lorenzo Pietro (and thereafter, a daughter, Josephine). All of them were sent to St. Mary's Catholic school, even though they were dirt poor, Pietro having saved his pennies from working the brickyards to make sure God would be their teacher.

Dad had one pair of shoes and a couple pairs of pants. He once told me the best clothes he ever wore was when he enlisted in the service and they gave him his GI-issue fatigues at boot camp. The clothes he wore on D-Day were better than anything he had back home. That's why he was obsessed with what was his. When we were kids, we had to take care of our stuff because he taught us that. He would say, "You're lucky to have it." That "it" could be just about anything.

When they played ball back then, they had to use balled-up string and broomsticks as bats. They had little but pride and fire. When they would play teams of rich kids in nice uniforms, they'd go out and kick their butts. It's no surprise that his favorite player was Joe Medwick, "Ducky Joe" of yore, during the hometown Cardinals' brawling "Gashouse Gang" era. Built as he was, like a pit bull had mated with a fireplug, and with his blend of talents, Dad excelled in all sports. In fact, he could have been a soccer player if he wanted. He could move, like another of those Gashouse Gang greats, Frankie "The Ford- ham Flash" Frisch. As a teenager, Dad played on a soccer team from which four of his teammates were chosen to play on the 1940 US team that beat England in the World Cup. He was that good.

But baseball was his ticket, and the subject of clashes between Pietro and Lawdie. Pietro even had a priest try to talk him out of playing sports. No son of his, no first-generation American son of his, was going to waste his life playing kids' games. Even the strictest fathers will play catch with their sons; it's a ritual of father-son bonding. But I doubt Pietro ever even picked up a ball, much less played catch with any of his sons.

LARRY: There obviously was a lot of Pietro in Dad. Even though Dad made his living in baseball, proved to Pietro how good being an athlete could be, he didn't play catch with us in the backyard more than a few times. It just wasn't what a father did. Maybe he thought it would reduce him in our eyes as a disciplinarian. Baseball was his job; he didn't bring it home, where he was a dad, not a Yankee.

Dad had to defy Pietro, had to sneak out and play, but always had to be home on time to work. Pietro got jobs for him, such as working in a coal yard and driving a Pepsi-Cola truck when he turned sixteen. He made around $25 a week, good money. Which all went to Pietro.

> **LARRY:** It's funny how things repeat. At sixteen, I took a job unloading freight cars for some extra money. That was the kind of thing Dad did back on the Hill when he was that age. Again, apples and tree.

But the jobs went to waste because Dad would sneak away early to play ball, getting himself fired. But what could Pietro do? He had been able to tell Uncle Tony—who they called Lefty and who Dad said was a better ballplayer than he was, a big power hitter—to stop playing and go to work. But now Uncle Tony and Uncle Mike were urging Pietro to ease up. As Yogi once recalled, "My dad was an immigrant who wanted me to get a paycheck. But my older brothers pleaded for me: 'Pop, we're all working. Give him a chance to play.'"

Already, big-league scouts were watching him at his American Legion games. He was easy to spot then. While small, he played ferociously, taking gambles on the base paths, pounding his fist into his mitt, taking charge. In one of the few pictures of him back then, he's crossing the plate on a steal of home, coming in standing having so fooled the other team that the pitcher never even threw home—and his own teammate in the batter's box had to corkscrew out of the way of the Yogi freight train. As he scores, his hat having blown off, his mane of long, wavy black hair flies in the wind.

He was that bold. But he also had that inner calm. Thus, his nickname. He didn't get it from Joe Garagiola—whose real name was Giovanni Garagiola—who lived across the street from him, a street now called Hall of Fame Place. Not that Joe achieved that status, but he got a lot of mileage as one of Dad's best friends and teammates. Both were catchers, and both smart enough to train themselves to be left-handed hitters, allowing a better look at right-handed pitchers, who are far more prevalent. (Another who trained himself to do that was Roger Maris.)

Joe for many years got the credit for coining the nickname everyone knew Dad by, explaining that it was because he "walked like a yogi." But history has settled on Jack Maguire, who was on the same American Legion team with them, representing Fred W. Stockholm Post 245, as the man who hung the alter ego on him, even though the stories shifted through the years. One was that Jack, who later played ninety-four big-league games with three teams, saw him sitting cross-legged, staring into space deep in thought. Jack told Dad, "You look like a yogi." Another was that Jack and Dad had gone to a movie in which there was some sort of yogi character, and when they came out, Jack hung the name on him. Dad, however, made it a real guessing game, saying years later that it was another Legion teammate, Bobby Hoffman, who did it.

Whoever it was, he did more than create a nickname; he created an American icon.

Joe, with his moon face and joking manner, got a lot of attention, but Dad was the boss, the strong, silent leader. He decided what games they were going to play. Being that these games were in St. Louis, the best players came under the eye of Branch Rickey, the Cardinals' genius general manager who'd pioneered the baseball farm system and built the Gashouse Gang. Dad was his kind of player. But Rickey was about to leave the Cardinals to become the president and GM of the Brooklyn Dodgers. Wanting to save Dad for them, he played a shell game, signing Joe in '42 to a five-hundred-dollar contract so he could shield Dad and sign him the next year.

Had that happened, it might have meant Yogi Berra and not Roy Campanella would have been behind the plate for the Brooklyn Dodgers all those years. We can only guess how history would have been changed. But it didn't go down like that because the Yankees were too sharp. They saw through Rickey's ploy and offered to sign Dad, but for less than $500. Dad wasn't okay with that. He told the Yankees, "Unless you give me what they gave Joe, I'm not signing." And they did.

The hard part was getting Pietro to agree. Dad could make more driving his truck, and Pietro didn't want his seventeen-year-old son traveling far from home. Dad's brothers begged Pietro to let him go. "You didn't let us go. Let him go," Uncle Tony told him. Papa Pietro and Mama Paolina gave in, on the condition that Dad had to send money home from his paycheck, which was like $50 a month. So in '43, off he went to the Yankees' minor league team, Norfolk, in the Piedmont League, where he promptly got malnutrition from not eating. He was down to around 160 pounds and told Mama Paolina. She sent him money so he could buy some good food.

"Don't ever tell your father I sent you money," she wrote him. "You're supposed to be sending money home."

Believe it or not, Dad was so guilty about it that he never again failed to send money home—even from a GI's salary while serving halfway across the globe in World War II. After Pearl Harbor, Dad knew he knew he would be going into the service in 1942 when he turned seventeen. Being a star, much less a wannabe, didn't keep you from the draft then or, like DiMaggio, Bob Feller, Ralph Kiner, and Ted Williams, enlisting and serving in combat, laying down their bats and mitts for up to four years, interrupting Hall of Fame careers. For Dad, the timing of the war meant he would be in a uniform, and in combat, before he could vote or legally drink a beer, not that the latter age limit stopped him.

He enlisted in the navy and reported to the Little Creek training base in Norfolk, where he volunteered for amphibious duty on a "rocket boat," a small, four-man landing craft equipped with rocket launchers—twin 50s, they were called, a pair of 50-millimeter guns. Rising to the rank of seaman second class, he would be a gunner's mate, providing cover for landing forces storming the beaches. That meant he and his crew would have to float in place only fifteen or twenty yards offshore. At least the guys going in could get out of those landing vessels bobbing up and down, which made many vomit into their helmets and load their pants when the bullets began flying over their heads. Dad must have felt imprisoned in a tin can when he saw his first action in North Africa and then on D-Day, in the early stages of the landing on Omaha Beach.

That morning was exciting, he said. Although he recalled that rocket boat crews were, with dark humor, called by sailors "landing craft suicide squads" and LSTs, "large stationary targets." When they went in, the boat lowered onto the water from the USS *Bayfield*, it felt like the 4th of July "with all the planes coming over." Then their captain injected reality—"Keep your head down or you'll get it blown off." They had a simple order: shoot at anything that comes beneath the clouds. So they did, sometimes firing blindly. At one point, they shot down an American plane and then fished the pilot out of the water. He smiled when he recalled the pilot being pissed as all hell and telling him, "If you could shoot that well against the enemy, this war would be over by now." (I've cleaned that up quite a bit.)

But Dad must have hit some German targets, too. He was good at whatever he did. He also got hit. He came away with a big scar across his thumb, which was split open by a bullet. But he was almost ashamed to say it was a war injury, since so many other guys got hit worse, much worse, and many didn't make it. One who didn't was in Dad's crew. Many of the guys in those rocket boats felt like sitting ducks and screamed that they wanted to get on the beach. Dad, though, said, "No, I'm staying on the boat." The one who jumped ship got to the beach. He was shot dead.

Dad also saw action during the operation at Utah Beach and was given a medal for courage by the French government. But, although he would have been given it, he never did apply for the Purple Heart, believing he didn't deserve it. He always said the army guys had it much worse. The sailors ate well, had clean clothes and a clean bed, but the soldiers never had it easy. Another reason was that he knew Mama Paolina, who was worried sick every day he was away, would crumble into tears if she knew he had been injured in any way. That way, he didn't have to tell her. Neither did he tell her about the German shell that landed in the rocket boat and would have left pieces of him and his mates in the English Channel had it gone off;

bless the Lord, it was a dud, but too close a call for Paolina to have handled it emotionally. So Dad only told Pietro and his brothers.

When he spoke of the war years later, he was visibly shaken, remembering how he was surrounded by men cut down in the water and bodies floating in water red from blood, how he had to get bloated corpses out of the water and back to the battleship. He said that was the worst thing he ever had to do. "Horrible," he kept saying. As if in a trance. "Just horrible." Remember, he was only nineteen, a baby. That was why he would have memories of that day longer than almost anyone else who was there, which must have felt like a curse. I'm sure he had nightmares about it, but knowing him, he kept it inside. It's what real men did.

Surviving was the reward, as was returning to baseball, but before he came home he had an opportunity to visit the old country. He was involved in another landing, in Italy, and when it was over, he was given a furlough. Like Michael in *The Godfather*, he and a buddy traveled through liberated Italy and Sicily. In 1946, he was back home, in his blue uniform and seaman's cap, smothered with hugs and kisses by a family that rarely showed that kind of emotion. He was home in time to play ball again in '46, the Yankees sending him to their Triple-A team in the International League, the Newark Bears, which also had future Yankee greats Vic Raschi, Joe Collins, and Dr. Bobby Brown. Not missing a beat, he hit .314 with fifteen homers and was called up in September, even after missing more than two years, still a kid, just twenty-one. It was, in baseball lingo, a cup of coffee, but he hit .364 and his first two homers, cementing that he'd be with the big club permanently in '47.

This happened as the Yankees were rising again to the top of the pack led by the aging, and to many, ageless, DiMaggio. In Dad's rookie year, when Bucky Harris took over as the manager, Joltin' Joe would win the MVP leading the Yankees to their first championship in four years. And Dad would make his presence known. Bill Dickey, the Hall of Famer who had owned the catcher's position—and the number 8—for sixteen years (missing two of his own with the navy during the war), had briefly been the team's player-manager in '46, then retired. Harris began with journeyman Aaron Robinson behind the plate, but went more and more with Dad, who hit .280 with eleven homers. He ended his rookie year with a bang—in game 3 of the World Series, Dad became the first player ever to hit a pinch-hit home run in the Series, off Brooklyn Dodger Ralph Branca, the victim of another dinger, Bobby Thomson's "Shot Heard 'Round the World," four years later.

The next year, playing 125 games, he improved to .305, fourteen homers, and ninety-eight RBIs and won the job for good—though his catching skills weren't honed until Dickey came back as a coach in '49 and provided him valuable instruction. Dad was always grateful, saying, "I owe everything I did in baseball to Bill Dickey." He also owed him for that number 8. He'd worn the less eye-catching numbers 38 and 35 his first two seasons before Dickey relinquished the single digit when he retired, saying Dad was probably the only man he would have done it for. Dad also believed he had won his place on the team because Joe D took a liking to him, and vice versa, something Dad was smart enough to know would benefit him.

Dad was still Larry Berra to some sportswriters, but that quickly gave way to Yogi as his background on the Hill was spread by Joe Garagiola and Dad himself. As late as '53, when Dad came up to bat at Ebbets Field during the World Series, the public address announcer called him "Larry Berra," perhaps to get his goat, the way Mets fans half a century later would taunt Chipper Jones by serenading him with chants of—coincidentally—"Larry." By any name, Dad was a fixture. Bucky Harris and Casey Stengel, who arrived in '49, loved him because he was an amazingly consistent hitter and catcher. "He isn't much to look at," Casey observed. "He looks like he's doing everything wrong, but he can hit."

Dad was certainly Casey's pet. Through the years he would call him things like "my man" and even "my assistant manager." Getting as technical as the Ol' Perfesser ever did, he once said, "Why has our pitching been so great? Our catcher, that's why. He looks cumbersome but he's quick as a cat." Harris even said he thought Yogi would be the most popular Yankee since Babe Ruth. And he was right.

It seemed they could do no wrong with the new number 8. In '51, DiMaggio retired, and a rookie named Mickey Mantle moved into center field. Through that magic decade of the '50s, when the Yankees lost the pennant only twice, the formula never varied. Anyone could be a hero for a day, and the aces changed from Vic Raschi and Allie Reynolds to Whitey Ford and Bob Turley, but Dad and Mickey were carved in stone, holding it all together, getting the big hit, making the big play. Dad seemed to even get a mulligan every now and then.

Famously, in the closing days of '51, just days after Mom had given birth to Timmy, Reynolds was one out from his second no-hitter of the season and the Yankees clinching the pennant. Ted Williams popped up behind the plate. Dad roamed back— and dropped it. Allie took the blame; he'd gotten too close to Dad and bumped him, knocking him down, but Dad made no excuses, he just muffed it. Allie helped Yogi get up, patted him on the back, and said, "Don't worry, it's in the bag." And on the next pitch, amazingly, Williams popped up again. But this time Dad squeezed it for the momentous final out. It seemed somebody up there loved him. And why not? Everybody down here did.

I never met or heard of a Yankee who didn't. He played so many games because even the greatest Yankees—Joe, Mickey, Whitey, Billy Martin, Hank Bauer—actually told Casey it wouldn't be the Yankees without him in the lineup. They believed he was the key to winning and felt a lot less confident without him. Yankee swagger? Its name was Yogi Berra. Little wonder the World Series was his showcase. He never coasted, but when the pressure was on, he turned it up. World Series games are all about pressure. Those National League pitchers had no earthly way to pitch him. When I met Jackie Robinson, he told me, "Your dad was the guy we had to get out. Mickey got a lot of homers, but we felt we could pitch to him. We couldn't pitch to your dad, because he could hit any goddamn pitch."

Dad actually felt bad for them. He hit three homers off Don Newcombe in the '56 World Series, two in game 7, when the

Yankees beat the Dodgers 9-0—the final out of which was Jackie Robinson's final at-bat. As Dad was rounding the bases, he called to Newk, "It ain't your fault, big guy." He was trying to make him feel better. But he never would have said what he was thinking—"There's nothing you could have thrown me that I wouldn't have hit out." It was the same way Rocky Marciano must have felt when he fought Joe Louis and knocked him senseless.

How did he reach that point of greatness? Only God knows that secret. He seemed a classic schlub, an underdog, which made people of all walks and ages identify with and root for him. But he had remarkable physical attributes. You can't hit like him without having his low center of gravity, his hands, and his rhythm method—hold on, I'll explain that in a minute.

He looked roly-poly, but he stood five-eight, 190, with not an ounce of fat. As if made in a lab by a scientist with a sense of humor, everything about him was economical, no wasted space or movement. He was in complete control. Built so low to the ground, he was almost never off-balance or off-stride. People thought he used a big, heavy bat, because his short stature made any bat look big. But it was a thirty-five-inch, thirty-five-ounce bat, medium sized, and he swung it like a toothpick. Surprisingly, his hands weren't that big. They were small, but thick like his father's. His pinkie was the size of most people's thumb.

He wielded the bat like a magic wand. And he had God-given instinct and reflexes. He was no singles hitter—he had 358 career homers, 313 (or 305, others say) as a catcher, a record broken first by Johnny Bench (whereupon Dad sent him a telegram reading: "I always thought the record would stand

41

until it was broken"). But, as incredible as it sounds today, he almost never struck out, in one season only twelve times. These days, Aaron Judge or Giancarlo Stanton can do that in three games.

He was, as everyone knows, a bad-ball hitter. But, really, he was just a hitter, period. How natural was he with a bat? There was another reason why he threw right but hit left, besides most pitchers being right-handed. When he was a kid, he played in a ballpark with a very short right field line—just like the old Yankee Stadium. He took one look at the shallow fence out there and said, "I'm just gonna hit lefty." He adjusted his swing accordingly and, *bang*, he was a left-handed hitter.

There was no "book" on him; no scouting report ever had the answer to getting him out, especially in the clutch. He could hit a pitch in the dirt or over his head. Pitches you're not supposed to even swing at, he did, and he punished them. I once asked him, "Dad, how did you hit those bad ones?" He'd say, "Well, they tried to get me out with them. They thought I'd chase them. But I still got the head of the bat on them." Then, too, he hated taking pitches for strikes, wasting precious chances, especially after being called out on third strikes early in his career. So he swung. It was all matter of fact to him. To everyone else, a mystery.

LARRY: I remember going to the ballpark during the '50s, and I still have visions of Dad hitting a couple of home runs over the 407 mark in right center at the old Yankee Stadium. He probably would have hit .400 if he was in a smaller ballpark like they play in today. He drove a lot of balls into right center that might have gone out if it was fifty feet shorter like it is now. He made it so simple. They put too much effort into hitting today. When he took batting practice, he took ten swings and that was it. There are guys out there now taking fifty, sixty, seventy BP swings. Dad said, "I only do it for my timing. If I hit a ball out, I don't care." As long as he got his timing down, that's all he cared about.

Dad said the best pitchers he ever faced weren't Bob Feller or Bob Lemon or Jim Bunning or any other hard thrower. Billy Martin once told me, "You just didn't throw fast balls to your dad." You know who Dad had the most home runs off of during his career? Early Wynn, who threw super hard. Hall of Fame hard. The toughest ones for him were junkball guys. Not that anyone ever really got the best of him in the end. Remember, he almost never struck out. That was thanks to those instincts and God-given reflexes I mentioned, but also because he wanted to swing fast and quick, get his wrists in gear. Sometimes, pitchers would just give up and throw right down the pipe. His eyes would get as big as pizza pies when those came in. He also almost never broke a bat. He hit the ball right on the sweet spot every time. Dad only broke like two bats a year—I'd break two in a game. But I was subject to the laws of nature and physics. My old man wasn't.

LARRY: I found that out when I was catching in high school and in the minors. That's when I had a much better appreciation for his talent. We'd watch games at the house, and when there'd be a collision at home plate, he would say, "I don't understand why these catchers stand there and take the beating they do. All they gotta do is step side to side." He said he could remember only three times where he got bowled over because the guy and the ball got there at the same time.

He was so quick, so nimble. His instincts were perfect. He had a way of springing forward when someone was stealing home, without making contact with the batter, as he did when Jackie Robinson stole home that time. Twice on suicide squeeze plays, he fielded a bunt so quickly he tagged the bunter out then dove headlong back and tagged out the runner—yes, that's an unassisted double play. For most catchers, that would be impossible. For him, routine. But then, most humans aren't born to be catchers. He was.

When I played with the Pirates, two of the coaches were Harvey Haddix and Bob Skinner, who played on that 1960 team, and they talked about Dad all the time. Harvey told me about facing him in that incredible World Series. He said, "Dale, I tried to hit him once in the knee, just wanted to back him off a little bit. Son of a bitch. Had he missed it, it would have hit him right in the knee. But he pulled a line drive foul, right over the dugout!"

Harvey was lucky it went foul and got luckier still. Dad hit .318 in that Series, but the ball he hit hardest wasn't the homer in game 7 that gave the Yankees their short-lived lead, but the bullet he hit off Harvey in the top of the ninth with the Pirates leading 9-8. Mickey was on first, McDougald on third, one out. Harvey, being very careful, fell behind 2-0. He tried to sneak one inside, and Dad sent a rocket that first baseman Rocky Nelson snared on a hop. In one of the most bizarre plays

ever, instead of throwing to second to start a game-ending and
Series-ending double play, he stepped on first, taking off the
force, then looked up and was startled to see Mickey stop dead
and dive back into first ahead of his tag as the tying run scored.

Now, about that rhythm method. What I mean by that is the
way his body meshed. You've heard the old song "It Don't Mean
a Thing If It Ain't Got That Swing"? That applied to Dad. And
not just his swing. He was like a stubby ballet dancer, a Nijin-
sky on spikes. He'd take those little steps on the field, like he
was walking on eggshells. That way, he could instantly break
full stride into a mad dash. Even when he took his practice
swings in the batter's box, he had the rhythm—that ol' swing.
It was like a metronome, never varying. For most players, those
mimed swings are just a ritual to bide time. Some guys made
a show of it, like Rocky Colavito, who would menacingly point
the bat at the pitcher. Mickey had that halfway version of his
normal, powerful swing, his big back and shoulders seeming to
swallow up the bat. Dad took his practice cuts with an under-
hand motion like a pendulum, or rocking a baby in a cradle,
with a little upward spike at the end.

That was to get his timing into a groove before unleashing
his real swing. His anatomy worked that way, everything working together. As Early Wynn, the great Hall of Fame pitcher
who played for twenty-three years, once said, "Berra moves
right with you." Behind the plate, when he would return the
ball to the pitcher, he would bring his arm way back and throw
in a smooth motion. Larry's right about how he fielded a bunt.
He'd pounce like a cat, throw to first while seemingly doing a
pirouette, his arms rising after he threw the way a ballerina's
arms rise up.

45

Even years later, when we played golf, he still had that rhythm, just walking the course. Few knew his coordination was working this way. It was just Yogi's way. Just as his famous habit of chatting with opposing batters when they stepped in the box. Many people thought he did this intentionally, to disturb their concentration. Not so. No one ever played more relaxed and more intense at the same time. As I said, the Yogi-ism that goes "You can't hit and think at the same time" is true, but there's another one he could have had—"You can catch and schmooze at the same time." At least he could. If he distracted guys, it was unintended, but perhaps paid a dividend here and there. Even Larry Doby, one of his best friends in the game and a neighbor of ours in Montclair, became more irritated with each at-bat. In his fourth plate appearance of the game, Yogi asked him how his family was. Doby had had enough.

"Please tell him to shut up," he pleaded with the ump. "He already asked me how my family was—back in the first inning."

But Dad carried on game-long conversations with the home-plate umps, too. Lonely guys that they are, they appreciated the attention. If guys did get distracted, it was only because he would draw them into making small talk. Hank Aaron ended one such conversation with a line that seemed to turn the tables on Dad with what sounded just like a Yogi-ism. That was in the 1958 World Series against the Milwaukee Braves. Hank was an unorthodox hitter, the way he held his bat.

"Hit with the label up on the bat," Dad said, offering some helpful advice.

"Yogi," said Hank, "I came up here to hit, not to read."

◇ ◇ ◇ ◇

Some thought Dad playing left might be a risk, since he looked nothing like an outfielder, and a catcher's throws are geared to go ninety feet, not from the warning track to home plate. But he was such a tremendous athlete, could play anywhere, and proved it—even if Mazeroski's drive refused to come down to him. He had played right field early in his career, and a few more games there later on, and even a game at third base in '54 and first base in '58. The most errors he made in the outfield in a season was two—as a catcher, it was one hundred errors in 1,699 games, a percentage of .989. In '58, in eighty-eight games behind the plate, he made exactly zero errors. When one of the greatest catchers to ever play can simply walk out to left field—in *that* left field, in Yankee Stadium, which was as big as the Ponderosa and bathed in those treacherous afternoon shadows that got late early—and play flawlessly, you're not talking about a normal player. To Dad, in fact, it was a piece of cake.

"It was like a day off playing out there," he told me.

He wasn't normal, in any way. He was different from old-school guys like Billy Martin and Hank Bauer, whom he loved because Hank was the toughest guy ever, a crew-cut, gravel-voiced ex-Marine with a face like a clenched fist. Dad could take care of himself. He had a temper, usually when umpires would make terrible calls. Remember the second game of the '73 World Series, Mets against the Oakland A's? In the ninth inning, Bud Harrelson was called out at home plate when he obviously dodged the tag. That would have given the Mets the lead, and Dad was so enraged he bolted from the dugout and charged the ump, Augie Donatelli, who made the call while lying flat on the ground. Dad must have said a few choice words, not Yogi-isms, and was ejected but kept asking, "Where'd he tag him?" Augie patted him on the butt and said, "Right here, on the ass." And he hadn't even bought Dad lunch first.

Of course, his most famous temper outburst was when Jackie famously stole home in game 1 of the 1955 World Series, the only Series the Yankees lost to the Bums. Both times, I knew why he went ballistic—the calls were wrong. Jackie was out, don't even argue with me. And no one could ever argue it with Dad, who was never surer about anything in his life except falling for Mom. Not many remember this, but there was a near-identical play in the '51 World Series when the New York Giants' Monte Irvin stole home. It was close, very close, but Dad never argued. As he always told me, if you get beat, accept it and move ahead. But Jackie, he would say to his dying day, was out.

When ump Bill Summers signaled safe, Dad spun around and got in Summers's face. Ripping off his mask, fire in his eyes, he brushed up against the ump and, slamming the mask against his knee pad, spat, "No! No!"—among other things—following Summers backward as he tried to escape the verbal fusillade. Yet, amazingly, that time he wasn't ejected. As a player, not a manager, you have to stay in the game. And he actually held back on Summers, knowing what he could get away with. (Just for the record, Dad hit .417 in that Series and was robbed of another hit by Sandy Amorós's game 7 catch on Dad's drive into the left field corner.) In fact, though there are no official records in this category, I don't think Dad was ever thrown out of a game, at least as a player. As Casey would say, "You could look it up."

And I learned from that, too. I never argued with umpires. There wasn't an umpire who didn't like me. Every one of them

I was friends with and respected. I knew how to talk to them if I thought they missed a call or called a bad strike. Umpires are a lot nicer to you if you say, "That one was close," not "Bullshit, you missed it." They get so much heat, they hate that. They'd get all huffy and say, "No, I didn't! I didn't miss shit!" and then hold it against you. If I told Harry Wendelstedt, a great ump, without any rancor, "Jeez, I thought that one was outside, Harry," he would say, very nicely, "No, that one was good, Dale," and maybe you'd get the next one, and he'd wink at you and say, "Don't take that one the next time, Dale." That's one of those inside-baseball things Dad perfected. All the writers also loved me. I was very respectful, as was Dad.

If you do look it up, you *will* find that a Yogi Berra was ejected from a game—Master Yogi Berra, a black Labrador Retriever that the minor league Greensboro Grasshoppers had fetch foul balls and bats in his clenched jaws. It seems that during a game in 2009, Master Yogi did what came naturally and relieved himself on the field, and he was run by the ump. The team's owner, taking exception, explained that Master Yogi "clearly couldn't control himself out there." That alone can tell you the difference between the canine and the man. The human Yogi *always* controlled himself.

Not that Dad didn't *want* to be thrown out, at least once. I don't know exactly when it was, but Dad told me that during spring training Casey invited Dad to go out drinking with him, which is what players basically do during spring training because there's nothing else to do. They wound up staying up all night, and Dad crawled back to his room—obviously, there was no curfew for guys like Dad, Mickey, and Whitey. Well, the next day they had a game, and in St. Petersburg, where they had spring training, it was brutal, a hundred degrees in the shade. The last thing Dad wanted to do was catch in that heat, with no sleep and, let's say, recovering from the night out. So, he tried like hell to get thrown out. He argued every call, threw in all the curses he knew, but the ump wouldn't oblige.

"Yogi," he said, "you can call me everything under the sun. If I gotta be out here, so do you."

The World Series was his playpen. That was when he rose to eminence. Even now, more than a half-century since he retired, he still owns the record for Series games (seventy-five), at-bats (295), hits (seventy-one), and doubles (ten, tied with his child-hood hero Frank Frisch), and he is second in walks behind Mickey, third in homers behind Mickey and Babe Ruth, second to Mickey in RBIs (forty to thirty-nine) and runs (forty-two to forty-one). Getting shiny rings for winning those rounds became monotonous, and Dad was unimpressed with glitz and gaudiness, anyway. After winning five rings in a row (and MVP trophies in '51, '54, and '55), he had so much hardware he didn't know what to do with it—and there'd be a lot more to come. In those days, they also gave you a ring for losing the Series, as a pennant winner. So, he wanted to get something for Mom. He requested that the people who made the rings make a pendant for her. He did that three times.

But he never kept the tons of memorabilia collectors would later go crazy about. He just didn't care about preserving a bunch of old bats and balls and gave most of them away. Late in his life, he had no conception of what his marketing value was;

he would give away signed balls, or take a paltry amount to sign a thousand balls, leaving promoters to make twice that. That was when my brothers and I stepped in and formed a company to make sure he wasn't going to be ripped off. Since 1994, anyone who wanted to use his image or pay him for signing balls—as opposed to the balls he signed from fans, which he always did without regard for money—has had to go through us. I'll get more into that later.

No, he wasn't a saint, just a man who wanted to be a good Catholic but never tried to be something he wasn't. But he was a new breed of ballplayer who had no interest hiding behind racism the way owners did for so long, pretending that integration would somehow harm the game. It's appropriate that he came up for good in 1947, the year Jackie Robinson came to the Brooklyn Dodgers. He would have never thought of himself as a hero or a crusader for justice. But he had fought with African Americans in war, played exhibitions against the best Negro League ballplayers like Jackie and Satchel Paige. It took the Yankees until '55 to sign their first black player, Elston Howard, a catcher, which some may have seen as competition for Yogi. But not Yogi.

In fact, Dad and Ellie became the closest of friends. Dad did all he could to work with Ellie on his catching skills, not thinking for a second that it might cost him games behind the plate. Every morning when the Yankees were on the road, they would get up early, meet each other at around seven a.m., have breakfast, and then take a long walk, talking about baseball and whatever else was on their minds. Other times they'd do some shopping, just amble down the main street of the town and stop into the stores along the way. That must have turned some heads, the two of them like Mutt and Jeff, black and white, just walking down the street.

Dad was absolutely colorblind. He didn't even think of race, didn't let it cloud his mind. When Casey had to get Ellie behind the plate, Yogi, the three-time MVP, the best catcher in history, never objected going to play left field or platooning with Ellie at catcher. Ellie would even learn to play left field, so he could stay in the lineup when Dad put on his mitt—and it was Ellie who turned around the 1958 World Series when he made a diving catch of Red Schoendienst's line drive to save game 5, allowing the Yankees to win the last three games. And you know what? If that had been Dad out there, I think he would have made the same kind of catch. Those guys did that when championships were on the line.

Ellie's wife, Arlene, was beautiful and eloquent. They would come over to the house and when Dad was hanging with Ellie, Arlene would enjoy talking with Mom. Arlene always said Dad was special, that he made their transition to the big leagues a lot easier. Dad was also very close with Roy Campanella, his crosstown rival during those World Series against the Brooklyn Dodgers. When Campy had his near-fatal car crash that left him a paraplegic, Dad was devastated.

Of course, Dad was also involved in the infamous incident at the Copacabana night club in 1957 when he, Mickey, Whitey, Hank, Billy, and their wives celebrated Billy's birthday at the famed night spot and wound up in a five-alarm brawl with some drunk in the audience—after which the Yankee GM George Weiss traded Billy, claiming he was a bad influence on Mickey the golden boy, which wasn't exactly true. Mickey was a bad influence on Mickey. The brawl started when the guy heckled Sammy Davis Jr., who was the headliner, with racial insults. Dad, who loved Sammy, was more a lover than a fighter, but crude racism would make him go to war again, though Hank was the one who punched the guy in the face (and was sued by the guy, in vain). What's not generally known was that the Yankee party had gone to Danny's Hideaway bar first and were also loaded when they got to the Copa. The team kept that part quiet.

Dad's good friend and neighbor Larry Doby was of course the first black player in the American League. When he had played with the Negro League's Newark Eagles, he moved his wife, Helyn, and their kids to Montclair. Larry, a quiet man like Dad, was from South Carolina, and when Bill Veeck signed him to the Cleveland Indians in 1947, he was only twenty-four. Unlike Jackie or Satchel Paige, who was signed later that season so Larry would feel more comfortable, Larry wasn't as mature or as prepared for the racism he faced. When he met his teammates for the first time, two of them turned their backs on him. But Dad, playing for the enemy, went out of his way to greet him. As Larry said, "Yogi was one of the first players to talk to me."

Dad himself was only in his second year in the bigs, paying his own dues. It took courage for him to go against the grain, but to him a man's skin had nothing to do with what he saw in the man. Larry was smart, a Navy veteran who'd fought in the Pacific. He had character and backbone; he was religious and a great family man. Mom loved Helyn. And Dad and Larry became the closest of friends. I went to Hillside Junior High with Larry's son, Larry Jr., and played ball with him at Nishuane Park, in the "black section" of town. There was a semi-pro team made up of older black guys, and Larry Jr. and I would work out with them. They thought nothing of a little white kid running around with them. And it didn't even dawn on me until later on that they were a black team.

In Montclair, that was common. It may have been an upper-income haven, but half of our high school was black. Not once did I hear Dad or Mom make any comment denigrating the folks who lived across the proverbial tracks. For me, all I knew was that at the park I could get into games with Larry Jr. and guys who were great athletes. They played baseball, football, and basketball, and the games were like wars. It was a rush that these guys accepted me, wanted to include me, because I knew I was good if these guys thought so. I wasn't "Yogi's boy" or "that white boy." I was just a kid who could play. You had to be good to play with them. If you weren't, they'd say, "Get the hell out." Not because you were white, but because you couldn't play on their level.

I'm not saying we didn't have our racial strains and incidents. But it meant something that Larry and Helyn stayed in Montclair rather than move as he bounced around the baseball map, hired again by Veeck in 1978 to manage the Chicago White Sox, a year after Frank Robinson became the first black manager, with the Indians. Dad could relate. For both, home was in Montclair, and it was there they would stay until they took their final breaths.

The numbers don't lie. The 358 homers, the 1,430 RBIs, the .285 average—that amazing .400-plus average in the late innings. Dad won as many MVPs as Mickey, his three coming over a five-year span, and was the second American Leaguer after Jimmie Foxx to win the award back-to-back. (Mickey and Roger Maris turned the trick later.) Five times he had more homers than strikeouts; those paltry twelve times in 1950 in almost six hundred at-bats. He almost never made an error—not bad when you make 8,723 putouts. You can look over his stats all day and find gems: nine seasons in the American League top ten in homers (and nine in homers-per-at-bats); nine in RBIs; seven times in total bases; six times in runs created; nine times in slugging; eleven times in catcher's assists; seven times in fewest passed balls.

He played nineteen years, all but a token handful games with the same team. *The* team. Dad once remarked, "In those days, to be a Yankee, in New York, you were treated like a god." At least by the fans. If you want a gauge for just how much sports has changed, Dad's highest salary was $65,000 in 1957 (the equivalent of still only $566,440 in today's dollars). Agents? In those days, light-years before free agency and a real players' union, you were on your own, god or not. It really wasn't about money, though. It was about loyalty and trust. Incredible as it sounds, Dad signed eighteen one-year contracts. He was so confident in having a better year than the year before that he didn't want to take a two-year deal because he always knew he'd get a raise, or at least make the same. And because he felt the Yankees had been good to him, his last year he took a *cut*, to just $52,500. Derek Jeter in his eighteenth and final season, as a shell of himself, made $12 million.

Through the dynasty, the Yankees changed players frequently, bringing in great players as pieces of the final puzzle.

Great guys, too, whom I got to know later on, like Hank Bauer, Moose Skowron, Country Slaughter, Tony Kubek, Joe Pepitone, and Tom Tresh. (Elmer Valo, anyone?) But the core never changed—Mickey, Whitey, and number 8. They were carved in stone from the late '40s to the early '60s. And it was number 8 who kept them hungry. Bobby Richardson, the diminutive but brilliant second baseman who won the MVP of that 1960 World Series in a losing effort, recalls that after the Mazeroski homer, "In the clubhouse, Yogi was not emotional. Mantle was actually crying because he thought we had a much better team and should have won. But Yogi was already saying, 'We'll get 'em next year.' And we did, we won the next two years."

Dad finally hung them up after the '63 season that ended when the LA Dodgers swept the Yankees. He was thirty-eight, having played 2,120 regular season and a still-record seventy-five post-season games (all World Series; that was the pre-playoff era). He knew his body had had it after so many years. In the thrilling, seven-game triumph over Willie Mays's San Francisco Giants in '62 that came down to one pitch, he played in only two games. In the '63 Series, he made only one pinch-hit appearance.

What eased the sadness of having to quit was that Ralph Houk, who was moving up from manager to GM, made him manager for 1964, though baseball people said it was a big gamble. Some of those people were his best friends. Whitey, for example, said, "They gotta be kidding." Mickey's response was: "Yogi a manager? What will they think of next?" Even Mom had said she thought Dad might become a coach but not a manager, because he wanted people he worked with to like, not fear, him. But it was a challenge, and he never shied away from one. Leave it to Dad to make it so memorable. That summer delivered the classic Yogi story.

The team was struggling into August when, on the bus ride to the park in Chicago after four straight losses, bespectacled utility infielder Phil Linz pulled out a harmonica and began tooting it. Dad, up in the front seat, was never a harmonica kind of guy. If Glenn Miller and his band could have been there playing "In the Mood," or Tony Bennett singing "Rags to Riches," well, that might have been different. But he told Linz to stuff his mouth organ. Problem was, the bus was noisy, and Linz didn't hear him. He asked what Dad said. Mickey, being Mickey, said, "Yogi says play louder."

Linz did, and Dad erupted. He jumped from his seat and slapped the harmonica out of his hands, and would fine Linz $200, big money then. The sportswriters had fun with the whole thing, but it had serious results. The question that hung over the season was whether Dad could pull rank on guys he'd played with, his buddies, guys he'd kept secrets about, like Mickey and his drinking. But the "harmonica incident" turned it all around. In the final weeks, they just kept winning, ninety-nine games in all, and clinched another pennant. That got them into the World Series against the St. Louis Cardinals. Dad could match them in all but one thing—a pitcher who could start three games, as Bob Gibson did, game 7 on two days' rest. Dad had to go with rookie Mel Stottlemyre, who came up late in the season and was terrific, but Gibson had enough to win.

That series loss was bitter for him, coming as it did in his hometown. I was old enough then to know what his life was about, and I could see by my mom and brothers' reactions how frustrating and devastating such defeats were. But I remember that when Dad came home the next day from St. Louis, he never said a negative word. It was the usual front—"They got us" and "If you can't win a game seven, you don't deserve it"—and then, "What's for dinner?" He was the last man on the planet to start throwing things around and kicking the furniture. When he used to take me to games, if the Yankees lost, driving home he was always calm and even-tempered.

But maybe it was best for him that he lost and was fired in that weird shuffle, when the Yankees hired Johnny Keane, who had just won the Series managing the Cards. Because it was Keane, not Dad, who fell into a ditch along with the team. Maybe Dad could have prevented that, kept making lemons out of even older lemonade. The Yankee dynasty was on its last legs, and Mickey almost literally on his. Dad was going to ask for a two-year contract to keep managing them, at a time when managers routinely were given single-year deals. He was committed to them. But if the Yankees had any life left in them, it drained when he was canned.

Dad took the firing with his usual calm shrug. "What are you gonna do?" was his mantra. Everyone knew it was unfair, and what hurt Dad was that Houk, whom he had won championships for, had betrayed him. Houk said hiring him was his "biggest mistake." I wonder if he thought that when the Yankees finished sixth the very next season, with their first losing record since 1925, then when Houk fired Keane and came back to manage again, winning nothing in seven years. As Bobby Richardson says, "I didn't understand [the firing] at that time and I'm not sure I ever will. I think it was a move that hurt the Yankees over a long period of time."

Mom couldn't believe it. She and Dad took calls for days from friends in and out of baseball who were mad as hell and commiserated with him. But she had that calming influence on Dad. She never let him get too low. She said it might be better, that only such a sudden break could have pried him away from the Yankees, and now he could start over fresh with another team, not have to deal with backstabbers like Ralph Houk. "Yogi, you should just enjoy yourself now. You earned it," she said. As usual, she was right. As if preordained, Casey Stengel—who had been fired after the gut-wrenching 1960 World Series defeat and replaced by the ambitious Houk, his first-base coach—pushed the Mets' brass to hire Dad as a coach, really more for PR value, reuniting the two malapropism-spouting legends to build an anti-Yankee fan base out in the new Shea Stadium, of which Casey said after a typical loss, "It has fifty-seven bathrooms, and I need one now." The footnote of that season for Dad was that he took his last big-league at-bats, again, as a PR thing. He played in four late-season games, went two-for-nine, and when he struck out three times on fastballs, he officially retired. Even as a stunt, he had wanted to do well. But after striking out like that, he said, "I didn't go out there to be embarrassed."

The laughs and nostalgia were good enough for a respite, getting paid for standing in the first-base coaching box, clapping his hands, slapping Mets on the butt when they reached first base, which was a Mets rally in those last-place days. But after Casey retired at age seventy-five, things got more serious.

The Mets were developing fine young players, and Dad would spend a lot of time in spring training with the catchers and giving advice in the batting cage. The future was bright. He was indeed happy, while in the Bronx they were anything but. Mickey, Whitey, Ellie, Roger—they would call Dad all the time, just to talk, because he always kept them sane. Those calls were probably happier for them than having to go out and play. Ellie and Roger got a break when they were traded and got back to the World Series, Roger with the Cards, Ellie with the Red Sox. But Mickey would continue to crumble and retire a broken man with an alcohol problem that would only get worse.

Dad, meanwhile, was enjoying his renewal. Only four years later, the Amazin' Mets, with Dad in the first-base coaching box, owned the town. When Gil Hodges suddenly died in 1972, Yogi took over as manager—and took them from last place in August to the World Series against the Oakland A's, one of a handful who took teams from both major leagues to the Series, the bad part being losing in seven games both times. That latter season, of course, gave rise to what may have been Dad's greatest Yogi-ism—"It ain't over 'til it's over." I was sixteen then, and the times Dad took me to Shea were magical. Nobody squirted water on me, but guys would play catch with me before games. So I was a Met fan. People never believe this but it's true. From my perspective, Dad was a Met first.

I was coming of age as Dad was hitting his stride again, in a new phase of his career, just as I was about to embark on the first phase of mine.

CHAPTER 3

"Carmen, Let Him Go"

YOU MAY NOT believe this, but never did I brag to my school buddies that my father was Yogi Berra. They knew he was, of course, because of my name and because Montclair was like family to all of us. Everyone seemed to know everyone else. Dad was like an unofficial mayor. He would take us to the movies. We would be waiting in line and the proprietor would see us and come over and ask Dad if he wanted him to sneak us through the side door. Dad would say, "No, we'll just wait in line like everyone else." When we would be at the airport waiting for a delayed flight, people would start coming up to him and an airlines guy would say, "Come on, Yogi, let's go in the back room so you're not bothered." He'd say, "No, we're gonna sit right here like everybody else." Those are moments when I learned that we're not special.

That sort of interaction with just plain folks was why he liked to go to church every Sunday without fail. We'd all go dressed in our Sunday best, at least until my brothers and I got older and drifted from the rituals of religion. Dad didn't say, "You gotta come." That was one of the personal decisions he let us make for ourselves. Dad himself was a religious man, but he didn't wear it on his sleeve and never intellectualized it. Neither was Mom overly religious. Dad's mom, Paolina, was a much more deeply committed Catholic. She read her Bible and could recite the proverbs by heart. She went to church every day. She'd get up in the morning and head for mass. For her, it was all about God. For him, it was partly about being with people.

That was what made him buy a bowling alley with his great friend and ex-teammate Phil Rizzuto. Back in the '50s, there were bowling alleys all over New Jersey. The alley was the hub of the social scene. And so it was natural that Dad would want to own an alley, which they called the Rizzuto Berra Lanes. I could go there and bowl all day for free; that's about the only perk he would allow me. You know from *Jersey Boys* how the Four Seasons got their name, after being thrown out of a bowling alley in Jersey and seeing the sign FOUR SEASONS LOUNGE in the parking lot? Well, Dad's brother John ran the Rizzuto Berra Lounge, inside the alley, and before they were the Four Seasons the group came in one day for an audition. And Dad was not into rock-and-roll; his thing was swing, big bands. So when they sang, either Dad or John said, "Throw the bums out!" I imagine that Frankie Valli left, walking like a man and swearin' to God.

LARRY: Funny story. In 1970, when I turned twenty-one, Dad took me into New York to see Liza Minnelli at the Waldorf and then we went to the Copa—for Dad, a return to the scene of the crime. And guess who was headlining there? No, not Sammy Davis Jr., the Four Seasons. They sang "Happy Birthday" to me. That's what it was like going places with Dad. Everywhere he went in New York and New Jersey, there was some kind of history involving him. He left his mark. It was like "George Washington slept here," only it was "Yogi ate here."

Speaking of Uncle John, Dad gave him that job running the lounge because he felt a special responsibility to his family. He was the first in the family to be more than a laborer, and he didn't send money back only to his mom and dad but also to all his brothers and sisters.

LARRY: Yeah, he brought John in from St. Louis. He said, "You're coming to work for me. I want you to run the bar." And it was a real family affair there. Dad loved Phil like a brother—Phil was my godfather. And Phil's brother Fred worked there, too. They kept it going until Dad and Phil sold the alley to them in '64. What I remember about that bar was that it was shaped like Yankee Stadium. Dad, Phil, and Uncle John went to great lengths to build it like that. It was like *Field of Dreams*. Build it and they will come bowl. I did all the time. I thought I was going to be a professional bowler because at thirteen I was averaging two hundred.

Then, in a short span of time, Dad lost his parents, which devastated him, but he made sure all the children were taken care of financially. Nobody would ever be left wanting as long as he was around.

LARRY: It was so sad when Mama and Papa Berra died. Paolina went first, in 1959. I remember distinctly that she had diabetes, and it took her eyesight and both her legs. Dad would go back to St. Louis whenever he could, to take care of her as she was dying. Then, just two years later, Pietro went. I got the phone call and had to tell Dad when he and Mom got home from dinner. I told him, "Grandpa passed away. They said it was his heart." Dad shook his head sadly and said Pietro just couldn't live without Paolina; he didn't die of a heart attack but a broken heart because he loved her so much.

I remember him looking crushed at those funerals. He couldn't believe he had to bury both of his parents within such a short time. The whole clan was so close. And he kept them close. He would bring all the aunts, uncles, cousins, everybody, to our house. If they ever needed anything, he'd send money. He paid for their homes, medical bills, everything. Because Berra blood ran thicker than money.

Our house was an amazing place to grow up. In 1958, Dad only had to pay $40,000–50,000 for a fifteen-room Tudor manor on a half-acre. People would drive by and, not even knowing it was owned by Yogi Berra, stop to gawk at the place, which naturally accrued in value many times over. Mom and Dad loved it and would only move from it when all us boys were gone. It was his castle. But he was a simple kind of king, who could live large in a small, family-oriented community just across the Hudson River from the bustle of Manhattan. I always get a good laugh at something Casey Stengel once said when responding to the ridiculous notion that Yogi Berra was dumb because he said so little and had been called apelike.

"How dumb can he be," he said, "when he lives in a mansion in Montclair, New Jersey, has a beautiful wife, three kids, and a lot of money in the bank?"

Dad himself had a variation of that. After he'd made a commercial for Puss 'n Boots cat food, he said, "People say I'm dumb, but a lot of guys don't make this kind of money talking to cats."

The truth is, his intelligence had nothing to do with book smarts. I was never as smart as my old man, who dropped out of school in the eighth grade. But he never craved status. He liked the fact that the town was small enough that everybody knew each other. And the house was the hub. At Thanksgiving dinner, Mom and Dad would have over not only our relatives but neighbors. Kids would be running all over, and Dad hired a horse and buggy to take them on rides around the block. Anyone could get in on a ride. He'd stand on the sidewalk, gabbing with the neighbors, personally lifting kids on and off the buggy. He loved being around people, even people he didn't know all that well. He'd get in a conversation and it would go on for an hour.

He would also get restless and like to go out on the town every now and then with Mom, get dressed to the nines. He had sharp suits in the closet and always looked like a million bucks, but he lived frugally and kept a low profile. That was a product of his past, growing up, when he had only a couple pairs of pants and one pair of shoes. When he had the bucks and a big house, he would still wince if you used a different spoon to eat your soft-boiled egg than you did your grapefruit. He'd say, "Why are you using that damn spoon? Why do you make Mom do more work? You don't need another spoon."

Anything that he bought us, a bicycle, a new glove, whatever, you had to respect it, take care of it well. If he ever saw a brand-new glove he got you lying out in the rain, he'd pick it up and hide it. He'd say, "That glove doesn't mean a lot to you, does it? So I'll keep it." And he wouldn't give it back for a few days, make you miss it. Same thing if he saw my bike left out in the rain. How different were those times? Consider the kind of glove I'd leave out in the rain—a Mickey Mantle game-used one, because Mickey would switch to a new one and say to Dad, "Here, give this one to Dale." What did I know? It was just a glove to me, so I'd play catch with a glove that would be worth thousands of dollars today. If only I knew.

You'd think Dad would have driven a big shiny Cadillac or a sports car, just because he could afford one. But he actually was a perfect match for a basic model that got the job done, and saved money. For years, he drove a compact, a Corvair, you know, the car with the engine in the trunk that Ralph Nader later claimed was unsafe at any speed. Well, maybe, but Dad drove at a safe speed. He had three of them. He'd say those Corvairs don't need water; they're air-cooled, less trouble. He could get in and around traffic jams and not be late to Yankee Stadium. Mom had the snazzy wheels. She had a Thunderbird, then a LeMans. She was not a Corvair type.

But in his later years he went out and bought a Jaguar. Maybe it was his midlife crisis car. Except Dad never really had a midlife crisis because he lived into his old age like a kid.

He had the same sense of wonder and zest for life that he had at sixteen. There was never a time when the Yogi Berra I knew didn't like who he was and how he was living his life.

I don't think it was until he was inducted into the Hall of Fame that Dad saw himself in a larger prism. The ceremony was in August 1972, and what a class that was. The other inductees were Sandy Koufax and Early Wynn, and the Negro League Committee selected Josh Gibson and Buck Leonard. Dad had just missed getting in his first year of eligibility but then got only five votes fewer than Sandy did. We all drove up to Cooperstown, where he closed his speech reprising one of his most famous lines, originally delivered at a Yogi Berra Appreciation Day in St. Louis in 1972. Dressed in casual chic in a light-brown plaid suit and gray tie, slipping on his reading glasses, he took the microphone and began, "I guess the first thing I should say is I want to thank everybody who made this day necessary," his substituting "necessary" for "possible"—something that might be called existential. As the crowd laughed heartily, he allowed himself a sly smile, having known how the line would play. Another example of how easily he lived with the caricature people had of him.

I didn't know what he would say that day, but he did, and it was simple, humble, funny, serious, and, most of all, straight from the heart. As always, the redoubtable Mr. Berra. He thanked the Yankees and Mets organizations, which he said were "the only two organizations I've worked for," which were like family to him. He congratulated the other inductees. "And last of all," he concluded, "I want to thank baseball. It has given me more than I could ever hope for. And I hope that when I'm through with this game, I will put something back." Mom cried all the way through it, so proud of the little guy who did everything for her. And Larry, Tim, and I shed a few tears, too.

My brothers and I lived a charmed life. We played almost every sport in school and on the playgrounds, and we were usually the stars of our teams. The only one we never really got into was basketball; me, because I played hockey in the winter. Larry, who was born in St. Louis during the 1949 off-season, matured first and made his mark as an athlete. And the funny thing is that we were so into our own lives that we didn't realize how incredible an athlete Dad was until we'd see little flashes of it at home.

LARRY: One day Tim and I were playing wiffleball in the driveway. See, we'd take a wiffleball, wrap it with electrical tape to make it heavier and keep it from being torn apart. We'd stand thirty or forty feet from each other, and one of us would just whip the ball as hard as we could to the other. Well, Dad pulled up in the driveway, and Timmy was standing there with the ball. Getting out, Dad said to me, "Gimme the bat," then told Tim to throw him one. And Tim was what, about nine, but he never believed anyone could hit him. He said to Dad, "You can't hit this stuff" and wound up and threw it hard as he could. And Dad hit that little wiffleball clear over the house next door. I think that was when Timmy realized his old man was even better than him.

You couldn't beat Dad at anything, and he'd never let us. We had this pool table in the basement. In 1959 they had Yogi Berra Day at Yankee Stadium and they gave him this real fancy Brunswick pool table. We never knew that Dad could play pool. So, he picked up a cue and made every shot, bing, bang, bing. It got so that Dad was only allowed to bank a shot in, no straight shots. We said, "No, Dad, we're not playing you unless you bank it." Didn't matter. Everything went in. Couldn't help it. He was Minnesota Fats.

The games he helped us play were the thinking games. He was unmatched at those. He taught us how to play gin, checkers, Monopoly. But he still loved to beat the crap out of us. He'd say, "I'm not going to let you win." We would wrestle with him, Tim and I. We'd stalk and jump him. If we got him in a hold he would bite you. Or pinch you. He'd grab the excess skin and pinch it. It was hysterical. We'd all laugh about it. But when he let us up, it would hurt where he pinched you for a day. That man was strong as an ox.

My brothers were my idols. I followed them around like a lapdog. I knew I was good because I could keep up with them. They threw balls hard to me even though I was seven years younger than Larry, five years younger than Tim, and I could handle it. I was playing in games with them and their friends when I was ten. And Larry was an incredible athlete. Big and strong, six feet, two hundred pounds, he moved like Dad, the same catlike steps. I don't have the same fluidity and hand-eye coordination that Larry and Dad had. He also had the same innate hitting ability. You couldn't throw a fast ball by him. He was always the star. And it seemed natural when he became a catcher. But he got hit by bad luck. He was playing soccer when he hurt his knee. Not bad enough for surgery, and he's a tough guy, so he went on playing basically on one leg.

LARRY: I went to junior high in Montclair, then a prep school, Montclair Academy, where sports was pretty much nothing. I had to beg my mother to go to Montclair High because they had better teams. Mom had tried to get me to take piano lessons, just to get me to do something besides play sports. That didn't last long. I had to play. How many kids would actually want to go to a public school instead of one of those country club prep schools? Actually, I know one guy who would. The original Larry Berra.

When Larry left Montclair State after three years in '71, he was signed by the Mets. Dad, of course, was coaching there and would soon be the manager, but he wouldn't have pushed the team to sign Larry. The idea of nepotism offended him and his values. No, Larry earned it himself.

LARRY: What happened was, I was playing first base at Montclair Academy, but the catcher got the measles. The coach had me go behind the plate and the other guy never caught again. I loved it. I caught all through high school and at Montclair High made first team all-state my senior year. Even then, Dad didn't do much to teach me the position. He said, "You want it, you go get it." In other words, prove you can do it.

Larry did that in the bush leagues. Whitey Herzog was the Mets' minor league director then and sent him to A ball, in Marion, Virginia.

LARRY: I probably would have had to go to Vietnam but for a technicality. When I turned twenty in 1969, they had the draft lottery and my birthday was drawn early. After college, I was eligible. But I caught a break. At 1Y, you couldn't be drafted unless we were officially at war, and the Vietnam War was never declared; it was called a "police action." Otherwise, I would have gone. I had no problem going if I had to. In fact, I might have had to go in '69—actually, I likely would have been drafted twice back then, in the military draft and the baseball draft— if Mom hadn't insisted that at least one of her kids go to college. I said, "Mom, I'll go to school later, I promise." She said, "No, I want you to go now."

So I went to Montclair State College for three years, but I was like Dad. I had to go for my dream. When I turned twenty-two and didn't need a parent to sign my contract, I dropped out and signed with the Mets. I just had to see if I had a shot. I was a good catcher and a good hitter. But I'd already had two knee surgeries by that time, so it was going to be iffy. And Dale's right, Dad had nothing to do with them signing me—at least he said he didn't. But he was happy about it. When I hit a home run, they put it on the board up at Shea, for his sake. I hit only that home run in the minor leagues. You know who I hit it off? A guy named Ron Guidry. I tease Gator about it all the time.

Larry could hit, but he literally couldn't catch two days in a row because his knee would blow up like a balloon. In college, they played like three games a week, not six or seven. The knee couldn't take it. After three or four games in a row, he was shot. He was operated on three or four times over the next couple years, and in a second minor league season could only play a handful of games on Mets teams in Batavia, New York, and Pompano, Florida, and had to retire.

LARRY: It's up to nine surgeries now. It was just too much. I didn't feel sorry for myself, not at all. I gave it my best shot. If there's one thing I do regret, it's that Dad never saw me play as a pro. But I'm proud that he did see me play nine games in my life—and in those games I hit six home runs. Those were my thank-you gifts to him.

Larry having to quit was a damn shame, because he's an amazing athlete. He's like Dad. Even now, if you put Larry in a bowling alley, he'll bowl 250. Put him on a foul line and he makes ninety out of a hundred shots. Put a Ping-Pong paddle in his hand and you can't beat him. He still plays a hundred softball games a year at age sixty-eight. He doesn't run, he walks to first, and they have a Larry Berra rule: if he hits a ball into the gap, they're not allowed to throw him out; they give him first base, so he can get the respect he deserves. They won't even throw him out even if the winning run is on third. Now that's respect.

Dad was hurt seeing Larry's chance at a baseball career end like that. Not because it was a failure for the family name but because it hurt Larry so much and always would be the great what-if of his life. Dad regretted not being able to see Larry play. But Timmy's time to shine came next. When he went to Montclair High, he grew to be five-eleven and 190, and he was the most physically gifted of all of us, built like a horse.

LARRY: Timmy never backed down from anything or anyone. I was older, but he laid the law down to me: don't touch my stuff, keep outta my room. And you did. You didn't want to cross him. We didn't know what he might do if he snapped.

We were so different in personality. Larry was stable, responsible, Timmy completely the opposite, me somewhere in between. Timmy was mysterious, aloof. You couldn't predict what he'd do. He was a renegade. He'd go off hunting and fishing. There'd be shotguns and BB guns in his closet and squirrel and raccoon pelts draped his walls. Dad, Larry, and I would be in the kitchen talking and from Timmy's bedroom window upstairs, we would hear the sound of a .22 rifle going off. *Bang-bang.* He'd run down the stairs, pick up his kill, bring it to the garage, and skin it. The rest of us didn't do anything like that—outside of the war, Dad never fired a gun in his life. I think he saw the devastation and death associated with gunfire and didn't want to hold a gun again. It was good enough to watch a shoot-'em-up cowboy show on TV.

Timmy was our James Dean. He rode motorcycles, which Mom and Dad weren't happy about. But all they could do was say, "What the hell, just don't kill yourself on the New Jersey Turnpike." That couldn't have happened, though, because he was always under complete control. He was a hell of a baseball player, too. He could throw a guy out from deep in the outfield, throw ninety miles an hour. But he had a football mentality and excelled as a receiver. He liked to mix it up, ram his head into other guys' chests. If you want to know, he was kinda nuts, in a good way. People were attracted to him, girls like bees to honey. What can I say? Ladies like Berra men.

> **TIM: I wouldn't say I'm James Dean. I'm gonna be seventy in a few years, and I'm still trying to figure out who I am. But I'll tell you what. Being Yogi Berra's son feels very good. Only three guys can say that.**

We were all thrilled when Timmy won a football scholarship to UMass in 1970. Dad, Mom, and I would drive up to Amherst to watch the games. We'd sit with Frank Tripucka and his wife—their son Mark was on the team—then we'd go to dinner with them. At the time, Julius "Dr. J" Erving was starring on the basketball team. The football team was less well known, but under a new coach, Dick MacPherson, they started winning. In Tim's four years he broke school records for both kick and punt returns, and as a senior he had 922 yards receiving. He finished there as the number four receiver in UMass history.

The only question was his speed. NFL wide receivers were supposed to be blazing fast, and that was one thing Dad couldn't give us. The top receiver drafted in '74, Lynn Swann, was almost a carbon copy of Timmy in size but with blinding speed. Timmy had no idea if he'd get a call. In those days there was no televised draft. We sat around all day waiting for the phone to ring. Finally, he was chosen in the seventeenth and last round, 421st overall, by the Baltimore Colts, who were in turmoil. The year before, Johnny Unitas was traded, and they had gone 4-10. The coach, Howard Schnellenberger, drafted receivers for his quarterback, Bert Jones. (A side note: a twenty-one-year-old Bill Belichick, whose dad was an assistant coach at the Naval Academy in Annapolis, was a summer assistant, really a ball boy, with the team at the time.)

The Colts, obviously trying to get some PR mileage out of our name, threw a press conference when Tim signed, Dad standing beside him, beaming. Dad, Mom, Larry, and I were so proud. We didn't expect him to start, but he was great on the kick returns. But that season was a horror show. They went 2-14, and Schnellenberger was fired after the third game. We went to that game, a 30-10 blowout in Philadelphia, and I went to the locker room to see Tim afterward. When I got in, I saw Schnellenberger, having been told he was fired, crash through his office door and split. He couldn't wait to get out of there. And Tim got a raw deal the next year when the Colts cut him. He was pissed about it, and so was Dad, with reason. He'd never even been tried as a receiver. He then went to the New York Giants and was the last cut of training camp. The receiver coach told him, "Tim, in my eyes you made this team, but I can't do anything about it." The head coach, Bill Arnsparger, made the decision. He had built those great Miami Dolphins defenses for Don Shula, but he didn't know anything about offense. Timmy said he was a real jackass.

LARRY: He had a bad shoulder, too. I think he popped it out and they wanted to do surgery on it, and he didn't want to do it.

TIM: Dad was a little angry. When the Colts released me, I told him about it and he shook his head; he didn't say it, but he was mad. Good and mad. The Giants thing, that one really hurt, both of us. But it was like he always said, nothing is guaranteed. You can't rely on others to give you a break. You have to leave no doubt, and I guess I didn't do that. I think that was a lesson to Dale. He had to be the one to pick up the flag.

Tim said, okay, I gave it my best, now it's time to turn to real life. Larry had to do that, too. He went into the construction business. He puts Environmental Protection Agency–approved, nonporous floors in pharmaceutical plants so that if there's a chemical spill the floors don't crumble. He put a lot of thought into it and didn't just settle for the usual sort of construction. He was looking at the future realities of that industry. And Timmy, who's a fitness nut, built and for a long time ran a fitness place called the Yogi Berra Racquetball Club. And he still thinks nobody can hit his wiffle fastball.

Before my physical gifts kicked in, I had been handed down the morals, perseverance, and lessons of being a Berra, mostly because I saw those traits in my brothers. They were my idols in a more relevant way than Dad was. The sports stars didn't really grab me, but I did love guys like Bud Harrelson, Tom Seaver, and Cleon Jones, the first big leaguers I had any recognition of. I had met them when Dad was coaching on the Mets. In fact, our house had been like a sleepover party at times when various Mets coaches like Joe Pignatano and Rube Walker and players like Seaver, Buddy, Ken Boswell, and Jerry Koosman came over. They'd sit with Dad for hours talking baseball, and it would be too late to drive home and they'd sleep over. Then they'd get up, Mom would make them breakfast, and they'd go. I'd share waffles and a bathroom with Tom Seaver. You think that wasn't surreal?

In fact, Buddy is my all-time favorite player—with an asterisk, of course, since I never got to see Dad play. He seemed like the bat boy next to the other guys, but he didn't concede an inch. He usually batted in the eight hole but got a lot of clutch hits during the '69 miracle season when everything went right. What he did hitting eighth was an example I would remember. But the biggest reason I liked Buddy was that when Dad took me to Shea when I was eleven or twelve, I didn't have a Mets uniform to put on so I could play catch on the field, and Buddy gave me one of his, because he was so small and his uniform fit me. So he was my main man. He taught me the fundamentals of playing the infield.

I was seventeen in 1973 when Dad became the Mets' manager, after Gil Hodges tragically died of a heart attack while playing golf on an off day late in spring training. It was a shock to everybody, especially to Dad, who absolutely revered Gil. Rather than hiring an outsider as the manager, the team made a wise move naming Dad, because he smoothed the transition and the players loved him the way they did Gil. But he was so different than Gil, who was a stern and distant man. Gil never would have brought players and coaches home because he wanted his players to respect him through fear; guys were physically scared of him. Dad was the opposite. He was tough when he had to be, but he wanted players to respect him because they liked him.

As I grew up, my brothers were really my only idols, not any sports stars. They were the ones who I looked up to and followed around until I was old enough to hang with my friends, and old enough to take sports seriously.

TIM: Dad had never influenced me in deciding whether to play baseball or football. I was good at both sports and could have had a career in either one. I just wasn't into baseball that much. But at no time did Dad believe Larry or I were as good as Dale. He says we were better athletes. Uh-uh. No way. With Dale, Dad saw a future big leaguer as a little kid. He would say, "If Dale sticks to it, he'll be good." That was saying a lot for him. The most he ever said about any of us was when he would brag to his friends and say, "My kids are good." And we were good. But Dale had a chance to be great.

I played every sport under the sun and took it to the max at Montclair High. I'd bloomed to near six feet and 180 pounds. Someone said I looked like a cobra, all arms and legs, and I had Dad's strong wrists. I wasn't really built to be a catcher, but I could suck up ground balls like a vacuum, so I played third and shortstop. Again, Dad made it clear he was not going to be our personal coach. And that helped us, too, because it took the pressure off. I don't think there's another son of a great player who didn't feel complete pressure to follow their father. Take Mickey's kids. Mickey Jr. and David were overwhelmed with pressure.

Mickey was the idol of millions of Baby Boomer boys, the quintessence of manhood and sports heroism before anti-heroism became the thing. And Mickey was fun in his early days. It was when he got older that the drinking caught up to him. I know Mickey's kids struggled with the pressure of having Mickey as their dad. My dad was much more responsible. He cared more about living a clean life, being a family man. He was no prude; he could put away those vodkas. But I never once saw him drunk. He knew when to stop. He never would have wanted us to see him not in control of himself.

LARRY: Lord, how that man could drink. He only drank vodka but would say one thing to never do is mix. You don't mix. He didn't mean mixed drinks but having a Scotch, then a vodka, then beer. He said that was the worst thing you could do. But he could drink. He'd come in at six p.m. and say to me, "Get me a vodka." His drink was vodka on the rocks. He'd have two or three or four of those things and get up totally unaffected, like he'd drank Yoo-Hoo. None of us ever saw him drunk. He once told me why. "I looked at the ceiling," he said, "and when it started to move, I'd stop drinking."

He also never wanted any of us to think we were his "favorite" son. It wasn't a Smothers Brothers thing where one brother would look at another and say, "Dad always liked you better."

Dad made sure of that. He told all of us the same exact thing: if we wanted to play, we damn well better be good at it, because nobody would give us a break because of our name.

> **LARRY: Dale says he wasn't spoiled, but he was. He was the baby of the family, so he was spoiled a little bit. He was Daddy's little boy. Don't let him tell you he wasn't, either.**

Dad's advice was fundamental to life in general, but his wisdom had meaning applied to baseball. There were Yogi rules—I'd call them the ten commandments, but there were a lot more than ten. The first was be punctual—which meant, in his case, ten minutes early, or you were late, and you'd take hell for it. Then there was be happy with what you have, don't obsess about wanting more. Don't cheat yourself; always play hard and never look to take the easy road. Never dwell on success, and learn from failure. When other kids were just trying to hit a fastball or curve, I was already on a deeper level. I was trying to train my swing to get the best wood on any pitch. I had the ability to drive in a run from second base with two outs, or from first by finding a gap in the outfield. Dad said he never guessed what a pitcher would throw, not one single pitch, and neither did I. Even so, he had a general idea. Hitting is all about recall. Dad wouldn't know what he hit for a home run. He saw it and hit it. But he'd remember what got him out and set himself for it. Usually guys know exactly what they like to hit. They cultivate that knowledge over years and years, and they hold it dear. But Dad only cared about what got him out.

That's how he caught, too. He would know what got a hitter

out the last time, and he'd play a little mind game with the guy. Like with Ted Williams, if Ted would come up and it was like 5-1 in the ninth inning with two outs, he would never show him the pitch that he would use to get him out in a big spot the next game. He would give him pitches he could hit hard and dare him to do it. He was saving the out pitch. That was why he would tell me, "Remember what the pitcher threw that got you out. Don't remember what you hit."

Hey, you can't argue with success. He never looked bad on a pitch. I did. A lot. But I knew what he must have felt like when I was doing well and could hit any pitcher. What was more important was to be the kind of man he was, which was even tougher to do than hit a round ball squarely. He had a favorite expression, which was more of a warning: "You have a rope, and if you hang yourself with it, that's your problem." That sounds like another Yogi-ism, but it was his way of saying our lives, our futures, were in our hands, and we had better give our all, focus, be the men we had to be. As I grew, we made a habit of replaying a simple dialogue, which went like this:

"Are you all right?"

"Yeah, Dad, I'm all right."

"Kid, that's all I wanna hear."

That was all *I* wanted to hear.

There was never a time when I didn't know I was going to be a professional athlete. I don't even know what I might have been if I didn't become a ballplayer. All I did was play sports, all day, every day. Five or six sports at a time. I'd start by putting on my Little League uniform in the morning, and by the time I came home at 5 o'clock, I had also played tackle football in that same Little League uniform. There were no cell phones. Your parents didn't follow you around. Mom and Dad wouldn't know where I was. I could have gone anywhere. But I knew one thing: I had to be home when the streetlights came on. That was Grandpa Pietro's rule for Dad, and his rule for my brothers and me. The eggheads call that laissez-faire. And the freedom gave me some slack to get into trouble. Not much, and not serious trouble. But I could be a bad boy. I would egg houses, throw snowballs at cars, rocks at girls. I knocked a girl's teeth out with one of those rocks. I threw a stink bomb into a moving van once, and it stunk up all the furniture. I pretty much got away with it because Dad and Mom didn't know. I could talk myself out of trouble. I had that gift.

But Larry's wrong. Dad never spoiled me. It wasn't like I had a chauffeur drop me off at school. My first car was a used, faded gold Chevy Nova he bought me. I had to climb in the window because the door wouldn't open. He made it clear he wasn't going to get me a new car. He said, "You're lucky to have this." As I said, that was another Yogi rule—whatever you got, you're lucky you got it. Like his Corvair, he'd point out that it was economical, cheap on gas. "If you want a new car," he said when he bought me the Nova, "you go save up and get it. Otherwise take this and be happy you have it."

As I got older, Dad didn't care what I did when I jumped in that car, but I had to be back not when the streetlights went on but by midnight. If you started to ask for a later time, he would repeat it, more emphatically. "Be in by midnight." By then, I had stopped throwing rocks at girls and began wanting to do other things with them. Dad wouldn't say it, but I knew what he was thinking. I'd bring over a girlfriend or something, and Dad would say what a wonderful young lady she is, then add slyly, "She's good-looking, too." That was code. It meant "Go for it, kid." He'd wink and pull me aside as I was walking out the door with the girl.

"By midnight," he'd say. Translated from the original Yogi, that meant "Don't waste too much time before getting down to it."

If I put up an argument, his eyes would bore a hole in you. "Midnight," he repeated, in a way that ended all discussion.

Those diversions aside, my entire teenage existence was really a launching pad for my sports career. I started in three sports as a freshman. A guy named Connie Egan was my baseball coach at Montclair High, and he guided me along, though my favorite sport was—and still is—hockey. Love to play it, love to watch it. Played it since I was seven. And we had a great hockey team. I played left wing and could move, loved to fire shots. In fact, it was my hockey games that Dad came to the most. He couldn't make it to the baseball games because he had his own to worry about. But in the winter, he would get over to the outdoor arena we played in. He had his favorite place to watch from, standing behind the goalie. He didn't sit in the stands because he didn't want to be a distraction.

But I think he had a little psych-out game with the opposing goalies. I've since talked to some of those guys, and they said,

"You know, your dad used to stand behind me, and he made me very nervous." One guy who went to West Essex High said he put some snow on the end of his stick and flicked it at Dad. "Watch it, kid," he told him, and that was the end of that.

Larry's right about Dad getting up at four in the morning so he could take me to hockey practice at five. That was the only time we could get the ice. Dad would sit there with his coffee and watch me for an hour and a half, then take me home. He knew I loved hockey, and he always said, if you do something, you better do it good. That meant getting my ass out of bed. I didn't complain. I scored at least twenty goals every year. As a senior, I was All-State in three sports: baseball, hockey, and football. In my senior year playing baseball, I went fifty-two for one hundred—that's .520—with eighteen home runs and sixty-five RBIs. All in thirty games.

They treat you different when you do things like that. I would come to school and leave my books in the gym office rather than carry them around. Never looked in 'em. When we had a test, two days before it I'd meet with the teacher, and he would let me take it in advance. I'd get my C's and that was all I needed to keep playing sports. I was starring in *How to Succeed in High School Without Really Trying*. And no one thought it was unfair. I don't think it's because of who my dad was. I just think I had earned it, being the star jock. That's just how it is.

LARRY: Timmy and I had the same privileges. I walked into gym class, and my baseball coach was my gym teacher, and he looked at me and said, "What are you doing here?" I said we had to take the gym test, climb the rope. He said, "You have to catch today. You're not getting hurt doing this stuff. Go over there, pull on the rope, just lift your feet an inch off the floor." So I did that, and he goes, "Good, you got a B. Now get the hell out of here."

In the end, I had a choice to make. I'd played defensive back and wide receiver, just like Tim, received around twenty scholarship offers, baseball and football. I could have gone pretty much anywhere. Bobby Richardson was the baseball coach at South Carolina and he'd recruited Whitey Ford's son, Eddie, for his teams.

"You going to send Dale to play for me?" Bobby asked Dad.

"That's up to him, Bobby," he told him.

There was never any doubt in my mind about that. And I didn't see the sense of waiting three, four years before starting a career. I wanted it all, right now. Just like Dad had.

◇◇◇◇

The major leagues had their amateur draft in early June. There were some great Jersey boys on the board that year, like Rick Cerone and Willie Wilson. And, no, Dad wasn't about to pull any strings. That's not how it works with scouts. They're not going to do anybody any favors. Dad knew all the scouts, but they didn't do favors with Mickey's kids, who failed in the minors, so why would they have done that for me? I was good, and everyone knew it. At times, there were fifteen scouts in the stands staring mainly at me.

I knew the Pirates were high on me. They sent Gene Baker, who oversaw the entire East Coast scouting. Then came Howie Haak, the special adviser to general manager Joe Brown. Howie had been around forever. Back in the early '40s, as a traveling secretary in the Cardinals' chain, he found a young Stan Musial. When Branch Rickey moved to Brooklyn and then Pittsburgh, Howie was his chief scout, plucking an unknown Puerto Rican outfielder named Roberto Clemente. Howie was the most famous scout in baseball next to Tom Greenwade, who signed Mickey Mantle. He had signed to the current team Willie Stargell, Manny Sanguillén, and Rennie Stennett. And now he wanted me.

Howie was a character out of an old baseball movie, gray-haired, spitting tobacco juice, habitually getting up and walking around the stands. I played well, so I figured that if a guy like that was there, I had to be on their list of high draft picks. But I was still nervous. Maybe he'd seen something in my play he didn't like. Maybe I thought I was better than I really was. That draft day, I went to a luncheon for area high school ballplayers at a local restaurant, the Robin Hood Inn. There was no way for me to keep tabs on the draft. Again, this was the dark ages, no cable, no internet, no real-time coverage. I only learned later that Mets coaches tried to convince the GM, Joe McDonald, to draft me first, but they didn't. And Dad may not have wanted to put me under that kind of pressure or open us up to questions of nepotism. After all, Larry had been signed by the Mets, and Dad didn't want the team to be the refuge of the Berra family. I wouldn't have wanted that, either.

During the first round, one of the owners of the restaurant

came over and told me, "You've got a phone call, Dale." It was Joe Brown. He said, "The Pirates are making you our first-round draft pick." It was the twentieth pick, meaning that Howie really had liked what he'd seen. There's a picture of me that day wearing a Yoo-Hoo shirt, so I must have worn it for luck. Media coverage of it was mild, focusing on the angle that the Mets' manager had bypassed his son, which incidentally came only a year after the Yankees had passed on Whitey Ford's son Ed, a shortstop, in the first round. It didn't matter to me. And Dad, always Yogi-like, played it cool.

"I'm very happy he was drafted by the Pirates, even though they're in our division," he said. "If I didn't think he could play, I wouldn't let him sign. I didn't get to see him play but twice, but I only had to see him swing the bat a few times to know that he's a prospect."

LARRY: We were happy as heck because Dale was not your model-A student, so we knew he wasn't going to go to college. He did it the way Dad did, getting right to it.

I was thrilled to go that high. Besides, the draft order didn't prove anything. The top pick was Danny Goodwin, a catcher, who also had been drafted number 1 four years before but chose to go to college and never really panned out in the majors. Those who did came after, like Lee Smith (recently elected to the Hall of Fame), Carney Lansford, Bob Horner, Lou Whitaker, and Dave Stewart. The only position player who made the Hall of Fame from that draft, Andre Dawson, didn't go until round 11. John Tudor went in round 21.

In baseball, there is no truer reality than the one Jackie Robinson used as the title of his autobiography: *I Never Had It Made*. All of us that day had visions of the Hall of Fame dancing in our heads. And all but two of us would get nowhere close.

Two days later, Gene and Howie both came to my house armed with a contract. I didn't even think about hiring an agent at that point—hell, my agent was a Hall of Famer who was also my dad, whose adviser on all things was my mom. This was on a Sunday, and the Mets were playing at Shea that afternoon, so they didn't come over until early evening. I was still a minor, so one of my parents needed to sign, just as Pietro Berra had cosigned Dad's first contract. But if those guys expected to steamroll us, they didn't know Yogi or Carmen Berra.

It had to be uncomfortable for Howie and Gene, with a Hall of Famer standing right there with his son. I would think a scout would be uncomfortable trying to crack nuts with Yogi Berra. For a long time, Howie and Dad talked about old times, just like you'd expect two baseball lifers to do. They reminisced all night long, even during the negotiating, recalling hitters and pitchers from the '40s. It was like being at a reunion. But Dad didn't lose sight of doing right for me. He would never have been bamboozled into accepting a bad deal. So we all sat around the living room table for hours. Howie kept asking, "What's it going to take to get Dale to sign with us?" Dad kept saying, "I don't know." But Mom was more forceful.

"A lot of money," she said.

She had a number—$100,000. Hearing that, Howie laughed

and said, "Should I get up and leave now?" and "They'll hang me if I go back to Pittsburgh with that number." But Mom didn't budge. "That's what it is," she said. We took a break, and Mom served what Howie said was the best meat loaf he ever had in his entire life. It got late—in this case, not late, early—and, just like those Met players, they spent the night at the house. I have no idea if this is unprecedented or not. But it was clear they didn't want to leave without a deal.

I hadn't said much, but I was feeling very uncomfortable about haggling over money. I tossed and turned and in the middle of the night I got up and went into my mom and dad's room. They were sleeping, and I woke them up. "Mom," I said, "I really want to play. I don't want to hold out. What they're offering me I want to take." Dad, who seemed to think Mom was being overprotective of me, agreed with me.

"Carmen, let him go," he said, either meaning from home or to the Pirates—or both.

The next morning, around the breakfast table, we agreed on $50,000. That was my bonus, only $15,000 less than Dad had made in 1955 at his peak. The salary was only $500 a month, the standard minor league minimum. It could have been five dollars for all I cared. And so I signed, opening the door to my dream.

CHAPTER 4

A Work in Progress

WHILE I FINISHED school, the Pirates sent me the finalized contract with a letter saying I was to report to their Niagara Falls team in the New York–Penn League on June 18, the day after graduation. So rather than stay out late and party after I got my diploma, I packed, and turned in early. In the morning I called my brothers to say goodbye and had some breakfast with Dad. As ever, he took it all in stride. "Go have fun and play hard," he told me. "Don't worry about where you hit in the lineup. Don't worry about where you play. You're a good player; all you have to do is have fun and do your best." More Yogi commandments to remember.

I climbed into my old Nova—I had to, the door was still stuck—and headed for the place where newlyweds used to go, Niagara Falls. The team was in the Class A Short Season league, which plays only a half season, seventy games, beginning in June. It serves as the entry point for a team's draft picks, about half out of high school, half out of college—with zero pro experience. When I got there, I was the youngest, at eighteen.

They gave me a uniform, and two days later I was at third base in my first minor league game. My first at-bat, against Batavia, I hit a line drive over the third baseman's head for a double. Next time up, a base hit to right. I drove in a couple runs. It seemed pretty easy.

The minors are a trip, the dues-paying part of the dream. That uniform was the only one you got. Two, actually—one home, one road. You had to wash them, send them to the dry cleaners, but you couldn't do that on the road, so you had to go to the laundromat. And if you played a night game that ended after eleven, you washed it in your sink and dried it out for the next day. You would go through the season with those two uniforms, unless they got totally shredded. The minors are where a lot of dreams go to die, in the middle of nowhere, riding old buses with no air-conditioning that smell and break down all the time and living out of hotel rooms with one bathroom with a stopped-up toilet on the floor and bedbugs sleeping with you.

This was the "romance" of the minor leagues that they make movies about. And I loved it. I loved the fans and people around the team. Money didn't matter. We all lived in an apartment building, and we had to pay $65 a month rent. I'd have three or four roommates. We were literally stacked on top of each other. It did have a certain charm for an eighteen-year-old kid living away from home for the first time. But hanging over all this was that I knew I was too good to waste my time in the bushes. I was a confident guy. I had swagger. I didn't show it, because Dad would slap me if he thought I was acting arrogant or privileged. And, believe me, no one on that team would have let me get away with that. In fact, I never had to defend myself as Yogi's son—I defended myself as a first-round draft pick.

That made me much more of a target for bench-jockeying. I'd hear trash-talk—"Hey, Mr. First Round, this ain't high school, boy!"—and it stoked me. Because I knew I'd be moving up, before I even had time to learn most of these guys' names.

That 1975 season was a good one for me, but not so good for Dad. The Mets struggled all season and the team's chairman of the board, Donald Grant, fired him on August 5, after the team's fifth straight defeat. Grant and some New York sportswriters were still steamed that, with a three-games-to-two lead in the '73 Series against the Oakland A's, Dad had started Tom Seaver on short rest rather than saving him for a seventh game on full rest. But Tom didn't have it and lost, then Jon Matlack pitched game 7 and lost, too. Dad told me his biggest regret in baseball was not winning a World Series as a manager. However, contrary to what some have assumed, the decision to pitch Seaver was not his alone; it was a joint decision made by him, pitching coach Rube Walker, and the general manager, Bob Scheffing. He would always ask for input from people, not just decide precipitously on his own. And Dad trusted Matlack, too. He had a wealth of pitching experience. It just didn't work out. That was what bothered him.

The Mets plummeted in '74 to fifth place when everybody seemed to slump. Still, in '75, they were above .500, at 56-53, and nine and a half games back, much like '73, when he made them "believe" it wasn't over 'til it was over. Dad's reaction to the firing was a little more biting than usual.

"I could sort of see the handwriting on the wall," he said.

Referring to Grant—who Whitey Herzog once said "didn't know beans about baseball"—he went on, "Mr. Grant was saying there was a lack of communication on the team. But lack of communication? I've managed four years and won two pennants." You can't beat logic. His replacement, Roy McMillan, didn't rally the team; they finished third, at 82-80.

But being canned allowed Dad some idle time during a baseball season for the first time since he was a teenager, and he used it to come watch me play. He and Mom drove up to Niagara Falls then followed me to Auburn and Oneonta, New York, where the Yankee team played—and their draft picks were soon of interest to him, because he would go back to the Yankees the next year as a coach, bringing good luck to a team that had sucked since they'd fired him in '64. The first time he was there, I could see in his eyes that he was proud of me. Even when I was twelve, I saw it in his eyes. When he took me to Shea, I'd get to take a few cuts in the batting cage against the Iron Mike machine and hit 85- to 90-mile-an-hour pitches. He'd tell Rube Walker, "Look at him, Rube. He's gonna be good."

When he came to my minor league games, people would gather around him like he was a circus act. So they put him and Mom in the owner's box, and he'd schmooze with the general managers and owners. But before the games, he'd come down and talk to me on the field. After the game we'd do dinner, and then he and Mom would hit the road again. Again, I never felt I was under pressure when he was there. I think there was only one time that a newspaper photographer took a picture of us. But I wanted to show him I could play. I hit a home run in one of those games, over the left field fence in our home park, which was 450 feet away. It was an old motorcycle track, and hitting home runs there was ridiculous. Nobody hit any. If you played at Niagara Falls, your low homer total didn't really count. So that was pretty impressive.

I know he thought so. He didn't get up and clap wildly like Mom, but when he said after, "Tough park to hit in," that was a high compliment. I would have never asked, "Dad, what'd you think of that home run?" And he wouldn't ever have answered, "That was a hell of a home run you hit there, hell of a shot." He would say something like, "Good hitting there, kid." It never got any more technical.

We had some good players, and three made it to the show for more than a cup of coffee, me and pitchers Al Holland (who had his best years with the Philadelphia Phillies) and Bryan Clark (though not until 1981 with the Seattle Mariners). By contrast, the Yankee team in Oneonta had nine who did, but nobody who stuck beyond a few years (the one who lasted the longest, Willie Upshaw, had his best years with the Toronto Blue Jays). We went 29-40, in fifth place out of six teams, but while I didn't hit great—.254—I led the league with forty-nine RBIs and won the Statler award, which the local sportswriters gave to the player they thought would have the most successful major league career. What I had to work on was my fielding—I made twenty-four errors in sixty-seven games. But if you hit enough, baseball people won't hold your fielding against you. They'll find a place for you.

In September, I came back home to Montclair. Usually, that was the month Dad's teams were driving for a pennant. I could see he missed that—how many autumns had he owned in his day?—and that he was definitely ready to get back to the game. And so was I. Evaluating myself, I thought I could play in the big leagues right now, at nineteen. I had kind of a baby face and thought maybe growing a mustache would make me look older. But reality kicked in when I went to spring training at the Pirates' Bradenton, Florida, camp and was assigned to their higher-class A ball team in Charleston, South Carolina, the Patriots. This was the Western Carolinas League, a much stiffer challenge. The competition was fierce. We would practice against Double-A teams, and they'd really work you hard. And, again, never once did I hear, "Let's see what Yogi Berra's kid has." It was about numbers. It was about when you were drafted and whose place are you going to take coming up, jumping over the people in front of you. I still had a few to hurdle.

Now, when I watch *Bull Durham* it all feels very familiar to me. That was the meat and potatoes of A ball. Charleston was the definition of the bush leagues. The buses again broke down and had no air-conditioning. The money was still peanuts. They wanted to pay me $525 a month, a twenty-five-dollar raise. You would get the contract, and there was a section for you to add comments if you didn't sign it. So I sent it back unsigned and wrote, "I won the player to go the furthest award, and I think I deserve $550 a month." That's what I held out for—a whole twenty-five bucks. I was going to have to pay $90 a month in rent, so $25 would merely cover the higher rent. Two weeks later, they sent another contract with the same amount, $525. They told me, "This is all we're offering, take it or leave it." I called Dad, hoping he would encourage me. I hoped wrong.

"What are you going to do, fight about twenty-five dollars a month?" he said, which helps explain why he made so much less than Mickey; whereas Mickey held out to get his hundred grand, Dad just never wanted to rock the boat. So I took his advice and reluctantly signed.

On brutally hot nights, we slept in the luggage racks on top of the seats. I'd been warned by guys who'd played on the team, "Wait 'til you see the locker room there." When I saw it, I looked for a floor. It had none. The floor was mud. There was no air-conditioning, and the showers had no hot water and leaked. Rats were running around. We had no team trainer. If someone got hurt, no one knew what to do. Those were the worst conditions I ever saw at any level in baseball, including the sandlot.

And yet, down in the sticks, I ran into some of my favorite people. Country rockers used to play throughout the backwoods. The Allman Brothers Band had a recording studio in Bradenton. They would hang out in the same redneck bars we did, so I befriended band members Butch Trucks and Dickey Betts. I would leave Butch tickets for spring training games, and the whole band would come and sit in the right field bleachers. They'd be in their shorts, tank tops, and flip-flops drinkin' beer, and you would never know they were the famous Allman Brothers Band.

One night in Spartanburg, I was eating in a diner at midnight, when Toy Caldwell walked in, the lead singer of the Marshall Tucker Band. I said hi, he just sat down, and we had dinner together. You wouldn't think a Jersey boy from the same neck of the woods as Bruce Springsteen and who loved James Brown, the Commodores, Cream, and Led Zeppelin growing

up could be a country rock fan, but because of those guys I
became one. Lynyrd Skynyrd, the Outlaws, Jerry Jeff Walker.
Makes me feel old, too, because almost all those good ol' boys
are dead. Butch killed himself with a gunshot to the head.
You wonder what made it all go wrong for a guy like that, who
seemed to have it all. But life never promises you anything,
especially happiness.

The Charleston manager, Mike Ryan, a former catcher
who'd played for the Boston Red Sox and Philadelphia Phillies, was in his second year at the helm; the first year, he went
45-96, buried in the basement—*thirty-six and a half* games out.
A ruddy-faced Irishman, he was a red-ass, which is what players called a tough guy. He had a dog named Harp, which in
Mike's New England accent sounded like "Hop." We all called
him Hop, thinking that was his name, until one day I saw his
dog tag. But Mike left his mark on his players. He believed
injuries were a crutch to slack off; if you could walk, you played.

We were a bunch of young kids, high school and college.
Al Holland and Bryan Clark also moved up to that team, and
some other good future big leaguers came off it. Like me, Don
Robinson and Tony Peña were just nineteen. I'd make it to the
big club before either of them. But Big Don was the hardest
thrower in the league. He could throw it through a brick wall,
or over it—he had twelve wild pitches that season—and pitched
for fifteen years in the bigs. And Tony couldn't hit a lick then,
but he would bloom and wind up playing eighteen big-league
seasons as one of the finest catchers in the game. Shortstop
Nelson Norman, the baby of the team at eighteen, would eventually be claimed and brought up by the Texas Rangers.

Meanwhile, I played every game, every inning, at third. I

made forty-one errors—that part of my game was a work in progress—but during those 139 games Mike told me I was the Pirates' third baseman of the future. Dad said he'd heard good things about me from baseball people—and, again, it had absolutely nothing to do with him saying what I wanted to hear, just the facts. For sure, my bat was ready and itchy for major league pitching. I hit .298, sixteen homers, a team-high eighty-nine RBIs. And I did that for another terrible team, though we made it a little easier for Mike by going 59-80 and moving "up" to third place.

I turned twenty that fall, not a kid anymore. I had a serious girlfriend back home and wanted to keep progressing through the minor leagues. The country was settling down after Vietnam and Watergate. A smiling peanut farmer from Georgia was president. It was as if my maturation was peaking just in time for a new generation, including new young stars in sports. I knew the Pirates were high on me, and when I got to Bradenton for spring training, I didn't get farmed out right away. Chuck Tanner—who had just become the manager after the legendary Danny Murtaugh retired—got me into a few games, and suddenly I was a story in the press. I remember Chuck saying in one of the articles, "Dale's got a chance to make a lot of money in this game." He also said, "He's a lot better looking than his dad, he runs better and plays third base better than Yogi ever did," adding, "And if he hits like his old man he will be in the Hall of Fame, too."

When we played the Yankees, Chuck made sure I was in

the starting lineup, playing third base. Billy Martin, who was managing them, got in on the fun that day. After I lined a hard single off Catfish Hunter, Billy yelled at me, "I started to order Catfish to knock you down, but I suddenly remembered I know your mother." I could understand that. Billy wasn't afraid of many people, but Mom put the fear of God in everyone. I was not averse to joining in the fun—asked if it was difficult being Yogi's son, I cracked, "After nineteen years, I'm used to it"—but I was a little bold, too. About being snubbed by the Mets and Yankees, I said, "If they didn't want me, I didn't want them." I meant, it, too.

Dad was also blunt, saying it would be better for me to play every day in Triple-A rather than stay with the Pirates and sit on the bench. Chuck thought so, as well, but he made it sound like I had a job waiting in Pittsburgh. That was Chuck. They called him "Mr. Sunshine" and he was the most optimistic and supportive manager I ever played for. Like Dad, he'd been in the baseball bloodstream since 1946. And he had his baubles of wisdom, too. "The greatest feeling in the world is to win a major league game," he said. "The second greatest feeling is to lose a major league game." As a manager, his rosy demeanor was infectious, showing signs of great potential with the Chicago White Sox and Oakland A's. Chuck was from Pittsburgh, and the Pirates wanted him so much they actually agreed to give the A's Manny Sanguillén and $100,000 to buy Chuck out of his contract.

When I was sent out again, it almost seemed like a reward because Chuck sent me hurdling over Double-A ball entirely, to start the season in Triple-A, with the Columbus Clippers in the International League. This was literally one step beneath the big leagues, the exact step taken by my father in 1946 from Newark to the Bronx. The Clippers had just become the Pirates' Triple-A team, at least for that and the following season, after which the Yankees took it over. I didn't need to hold out this time. They bumped me up to $750 a month. I said, "Holy shit, this is big money." Okay, I was still a little naïve, but I was learning about a lot of things.

The manager there was a spunky guy named Johnny Lipon, who had played shortstop for four big-league teams over nine seasons back in the '40s and '50s and then turned to managing, in '71, as interim skipper for the Cleveland Indians. Lip was a great guy, another baseball lifer. And my Lord, the talent we had. The guy I had to beat out at third base was Ken Macha, and we really pushed each other—he hit .335, I hit .290, though I would start all but four games. Kenny was a real mover; he played forever in the minors, all around the diamond, got into 180 games over the course of six seasons in the majors, went to Japan, and came back to win over ninety games three times in four years managing the Oakland A's and two lesser years managing the Milwaukee Brewers.

Several guys would get promoted to the Pirates—Steve Nicosia, Al Holland, Don Robinson, Mike "Hit Man" Easler, and two others we'll run across in much different contexts later in this story, Rod Scurry and Ed Whitson. Ex–big leaguers Bob Oliver and Jim Nettles, Graig's brother, were hanging on, fighting the clock. Several others would get called up with other teams. So the scent of the majors was strong all summer. And I was ready. It was crazy. I'd jumped over everybody in the Pirates' minor league system just that season. That's how good I was. Forget about pretty good; I was the best prospect in the Pirates organization, the best minor league prospect in the country. Triple-A is filled with the best prospects, and I was better than all of them. That was just a fact.

I was going to be called up in September when the minor league season ended. But the Pirates were in a tight race, only two games behind the Philadelphia Phillies, when on August 21 their second baseman Rennie Stennett broke his leg on a slide into second. Chuck needed infield help, and the next day I was called up. At the time, I was leading the league in home runs with eighteen and fifty-four RBIs. I'd cut my errors to twenty-nine, and my fielding percentage was 92 percent. I was ready.

I called Mom and Dad immediately and told them I got called to the big leagues. Dad was actually excited. "Goddamn, that's great," he said. "This is the big time." Mom was so excited she was crying. Larry and Tim were slapping high fives. Of course, Tim had known what it was to play in a big league, and both had seen their careers crash and burn too soon. But neither had any jealousy that I might go further—they wanted that more than anything. They never talked about what might have been. All they knew was that they could brag on their little bro.

TIM: It's like I say, Dale was always the best athlete among us, despite what he says. He was the one who was going to go furthest. It almost seemed predestined. Larry and I were good athletes, but we never kidded our-selves. We were marginal. We went to school to be able to have a fallback. Dale had no other fallback. He went to school to play ball. He had no other interests. It was all or nothing.

I flew into Pittsburgh and two days later, Monday, August 22, 1977, I found myself in the starting lineup under the lights at Three Rivers Stadium. At twenty, the second youngest player in the National League, I was officially the 11,537th man to play in the big leagues—thirty years after my dad became the 7,927th. I remember when I walked into the stadium how enormous it looked. I felt like an ant. The stands were triple-decked in a perfect circle all around the field. They swallowed you up. You couldn't see anything but concrete and seats, not the beautiful scenery outside, the rivers, the bridges, the downtown skyscrapers. A lot of ballparks have a fun atmosphere, but Three Rivers was dark and foreboding. Still, walking into a big-league clubhouse was not intimidating to me. I'd done it countless times before as a kid.

The game that night was against the San Diego Padres. Batting sixth, my first at-bat came in the bottom of the second, with no outs, Al Oliver on first. I saw the ball well out of Bob Shirley's hand but didn't get enough wood on it, lifting a fly ball to left. After that, I grounded out and popped out. When my turn came up again in the bottom of the ninth, we were down 1-0 and Chuck pinch-hit for me. I understood why. I would have had to go up there against the handlebar-mustached Rollie Fingers, perhaps the best relief pitcher of all time. But that didn't mean I wasn't disappointed, more so when Ed Ott flew out and Duffy Dyer struck out to end it.

Dad said, "Hey, that's how it goes in baseball. You can't play what-if. You turn the page." The next night, I went zero-for-three, with a walk in another close game, and again Chuck pinch-hit for me, in the seventh when Oliver singled with two outs. We were down 5-4. Omar Moreno, in my place, grounded out. But when Al blasted a homer, Mazeroski-style, leading off the bottom of the ninth, personal disappointment faded away. Being in a pennant race was what baseball is all about, not one's own stats. Or money. When you get called up, you get a pro-rated share of baseball minimum salary, which at the time was $17,500. So I went from $750 a month to about twice that.

Yet I felt like I would play for free if I could watch Stargell, Oliver, Parker, Bill Robinson, and all the other veterans stay so focused each day, each at-bat, never getting down after a loss. That was a priceless education. All of them made me feel at home. Willie was the most amazing man I've ever met, next to my father. He couldn't have been kinder to me. "Pops" had been around since 1962, but he made me feel like an equal. He didn't care if you were a rookie or a veteran. He wouldn't let you get down on yourself. He took it as his job as the team leader to make you believe in yourself. Sort of like Dad, but with a much more verbal, hands-on approach.

Seeing Willie hit—which was his ticket to the Hall of Fame—I noticed he and Dad were a lot alike. They had the same rhythm in hitting. Remember how Willie took his pre-pitch swings? He'd windmill the bat 'round and 'round. He was so relaxed he looked like he might nod off. Then he would pounce on a pitch, like a rabid lion. His swing was frightening. Yeah, he did strike out a lot—154 times one year—but he was a long-ball hitter and swung so hard it could cool the park off on a hot day. He hit over forty homers twice, over thirty-four times, 475 in all. He was so fluid he never looked out of sync. His whole body fused to create all that power.

Pops and my pop were the most respected players of their generations. How lucky was I to have been brought up by one and play with the other? To me, the greatest measure of their standing among their peers was that pitchers wouldn't throw at them. One time Dad was hit, and he said to the pitcher as he was going to first, "Are you trying to hit me?" And the guy was very upset at the thought. He said, "No, it was an accident, Yogi, believe me." Same thing with Pops. You didn't throw at Pops. A Drysdale or Gibson might throw him inside, because you have to with a power guy. But if a manager ever told them to hit Stargell, they'd say, "No way, I'm not hitting Pops." Hitting me, on the other hand, they had no objections to that.

The Los Angeles Dodgers rolled into Pittsburgh next, a big series, both teams among the best in the game. Like us, Tommy Lasorda was loaded—Steve Garvey, Ron Cey, Dusty Baker, Reggie Smith, Bill Russell, Tommy John on the hill. I didn't get into the two games other than a pinch-hitting appearance. I didn't play much the rest of the way. I got my first hit, a pinch-hit single against Tommy John, out in LA, but Chuck, trying to find the answer at third, began to use Ken Macha there. The Phillies left us for dead, even though we kept winning—we won ninety-six games and finished five games behind, but there was no wild card then. Amazingly, we did that even though Willie was getting old; he was thirty-seven and hurt most of the season. Bill Robinson filled in for him and hit .304, but Willie had more left in the tank. As for me, I did break out in one game, going three-for-four against the Chicago Cubs the day before the season ended, raising my average to a robust .175. That average got me another ticket back to Triple-A when the '78 season would begin. But Chuck assured me I'd be back, and soon. That wasn't just his optimism talking; he was a man who saw something special in me.

Other than New York and the Yankees, I don't think there's a better baseball town than Pittsburgh, or a team as entrenched in history than the Pirates. They go back further than the Yankees, having begun in 1881, and their blue-collar fans are the opposite of the blasé crowds that came to Dad's games in the Yankees' U.S. Steel era, even though, ironically, Pittsburgh is the home of the actual U.S. Steel. There were often a lot of empty seats, and years of losing, but most fans lived and died with the "Bucs," mostly dying, which is why the whole town exploded when Mazeroski hit that ball out of Dad's reach. They had won it all only four times by the time I got there. The late, longtime Mets' play-by-play man Ralph Kiner, a Hall of Famer, played eight years for the Pirates after World War II, leading the league every year in homers, but only once did they finish above .500, and lost 112 games one year. But where the club made its biggest contribution to baseball was in cultivating the first wave of great Latino players after Howie Haak got Branch Rickey to sign Clemente. That wave would lead to the majority of ballplayers today being Latinos.

It wasn't until the '70s that the working-class ethnic population of Steel Town were rewarded with consistent winning. I would watch Pirates games then and see the aging Clemente and the younger stars like Oliver, Stargell, Parker, Bob Robertson, and Richie Hebner. Dad would just shake his head. His Mets were a good team, a World Series–level team, but they were thin in the minor leagues. He'd say, "The Pirates come out on the field and they got Mike Easler, Mitchell Page, Tony Armas. Who do we got in the minors? We got nobody." Soon enough, I'd be among them, although I thought it was a little sad that the team had by then switched from those great old sleeveless uniforms to the yellow ones with the nonbelted, elastic waistbands and horizontal-striped, pillbox-style caps. We weren't Pirates; we were canaries.

Dad and I didn't talk much during that '77 stretch drive. First of all, he had one of his own in New York. With him as the good luck charm in 1976, the Yankees had gone to the World Series, losing in four straight to Cincinnati's Big Red Machine. But they were about to take back the town from the Mets and dominate the sports page headlines with the numerous antics of "the Bronx Zoo." In '77, my rookie year, he was right there when Billy Martin almost fought with Reggie Jackson after pulling him from a game in Boston for loafing in the outfield. Dad helped Ellie Howard, also a coach then, separate the pair in the dugout. The effect of that was something like Dad's blowout on the bus with Phil Linz; the team put it together after that, just like in '64, and Dad got another ring for his collection. And he was right there in '78 when George Steinbrenner fired Billy and the team went on a tear under Bob Lemon to repeat. Ring number 12. Both years, Yankee players said Dad was a major factor keeping them sane in that Zoo, the only rock of stability in a circus of daily chaos.

If the '77 season was like a rerun for Dad, that '78 season was like one for me. Back in Columbus, I hit .280, with eighteen homers and sixty-three RBIs and was the top vote-getter in the International League All-Star Game when I got the word in late July that the Pirates were again calling me up. The difference from the year before was that the Pirates weren't in a pennant race—or so it seemed. We were eleven and a half games behind the Phillies on August 12 after losing seventeen of twenty-one games, bringing our record to 51-61. And I didn't exactly help. I went hitless in my first twenty-four at-bats. That was brutal, but Chuck always wore his rose-colored glasses. "This may not be the end; it may be the beginning," he told us. And like Dad's '73 Mets, we believed. From that point on, I began to hit, along with everyone else. We became nearly unbeatable.

During that run Chuck had me splitting time at third with Phil "Scrap Iron" Garner and shortstop with Frank Taveras. He had me hitting eighth, which became a real advantage. Normally, the number 8 hole is where you put your weakest hitter. But something about it motivated me. From that slot, I hit my first big-league homer on Sunday, August 20 at home against the Houston Astros' Tom Dixon, a solo shot in the fourth inning that put us up 6-2. I also singled in the sixth and we hung on to win 7-6. Chuck then shifted me to the 7 hole, and I hit my second homer two games later, another solo, putting us ahead of the Atlanta Braves 2-0, a game we won 3-1.

But he liked me hitting eighth. I could drive runs in from first and second base. I could hit doubles. And I would be walked to get to the pitcher, so our leadoff hitter would be up the next inning. That happened twice in the next game, a 5-1 win. Was I as crucial as Pops or Parker? No. But I was a piece of the puzzle. After August 12, we went 27-14, winning twenty-four straight at home, going 21-9 in September and putting the fear of God into the Phillies. My biggest contribution was on September 3 against the Atlanta Braves. We came in three and a half games back, but the Phillies lost. Chuck put me in the game at third in the seventh inning when John Milner got hurt, moving Bill Robinson from third to first. In the bottom of the ninth, it was 3-3, one out, runners on first and second, Braves reliever Gene Garber on the hill.

I stepped in, hitting all of .171 but on a roll. Garber tried to sneak a fastball by me inside. I turned on it, laid a quick, smooth swing on it, and the ball jumped off the bat, a line drive not fifty feet above the ground that landed in the left field stands—my first walk-off homer, and the first time I was mobbed at home plate after joyously rounding the bases and given a bear hug by Pops. The UPI wire service covered it with an inevitable angle, leading with: "A pennant race and a guy named Berra. It's an old story with a new twist...it appears [Yogi's] son, Dale, has inherited some of the old man's flair for performing under the pressure." That was probably the first time many fans outside of Pittsburgh knew I was in the big leagues, and I played down the connection with Dad, though I equated our team with the '73

Mets, calling both teams "a bunch of young guys having a lot of fun out there on the field and winning, too."

It was my fourth big-league homer, the third over twelve days, with two more to come in September, but I'd never hit a bigger one. The win was our seventh straight at the time, nineteenth in the last twenty-two. Because the Phillies lost a doubleheader to the Giants, we gained a game and half on them. We got within a half game of them but were three and a half back when the Phillies came in to Three Rivers for the last four games of the season. We needed to sweep, but figured the pressure was on them. We took the first two, both in thrilling fashion in the bottom of the ninth. In the latter game, our toothpick pitcher Bruce Kison homered—off Steve Carlton, no less—and we won on a walk-off balk, of all things.

LARRY: We followed every game. We thought he was doing great and would do much better as time went by. We would get the Pirates' radio station, and we'd always have the games on. One time later on in Dale's career I was driving down the Jersey shore with my wife at the time and he hit a home run off of Steve Carlton, too. I almost drove off the road. I was screaming, "Atta boy!" I think Timmy and I were more emotionally invested in Dale than we were listening to Dad's games as kids. It's indescribable when you see your brother, who grew up before your eyes, make it on his own in such a big-time, high-pressure situation.

All of Pittsburgh was going nuts. The park was packed for those games. But then, we cracked. Pops hit a three-run homer in the first inning and we led 4-1, only to see the Phillies chip away. Greg Luzinski, one dangerous hitter, hit a three-run shot off Grant Jackson in the sixth to go up 6-4, and we couldn't recover. We scored four in the bottom of the ninth but fell short, 10-8, and were eliminated. We won the meaningless finale, finishing 88-73, crushed because we believed we had jelled into a title team. Parker was the National League's MVP, and Pops was defying Father Time, hitting twenty-eight home runs with ninety-seven RBIs, winning Comeback Player of the Year. Our starting and relief pitching were strong. We were, of course, a Fam-a-lee. And I knew all about what that meant.

CHAPTER 5

Ten Feet Tall

I COULDN'T WAIT to get to Bradenton in February 1979, and when I did, it was after a crazy experiment by Chuck Tanner. Over the off-season, Chuck thought it would be a good idea to send me to the winter league in Puerto Rico to learn to play the outfield. I thought it was a rare, ill-advised move by Chuck, and the Pirates' general manager, Harding Peterson, had to talk me into it. But I never really got my head into it, and after a few days I packed and caught a plane home to Montclair. Was I out of line, pushing my luck for a young player not yet established? Maybe. But I knew what my limitations were. I wasn't Yogi Berra, who could just pick up a fielder's glove and go to left field. Harding and Chuck didn't hold it against me. After Harding talked with me, he knew I was right. "Dale wasn't happy," he told the press, "and he said he couldn't put his mind on baseball. Under those circumstances, if he remained, it may have done more harm than good."

My mind was focused on improving as a hitter and third baseman/shortstop. While I'd hit only .207 in '78, when I got hot I blossomed, and those six homers in the stretch drive was a statement. I'd played fifty-six games, started thirty-seven, made good things happen. And Chuck took me north with the team to start the '79 season. I played the first two months, but not regularly. I would play shortstop when Tim Foli got a rest on Sundays, third base other times, but mostly sit. Then in June the Pirates made a huge trade, swapping pitcher Ed Whitson to get third baseman Bill Madlock from the San Francisco Giants. I never saw a better line-drive hitter than Mad Dog. In his previous six seasons he'd hit .300 each year, winning batting titles for the Chicago Cubs in '75 and '76 when he hit .354 and .339. He could roll out of bed and hit a scorching line drive into the gap.

That move solidified the infield. With Madlock, Phil Garner, and Tim Foli, there was just no room for me. Chuck Tanner could see I was vegetating and called me into his office. "Dale, you're going to be an everyday player in this league," he said. "But you're only twenty-two and I can't have you sitting on this bench, so I'm going to send you to Portland." That was the team's Triple-A team in the Pacific Coast League, where I would be playing every day, staying sharp. It was fine with me. I didn't like sitting and watching. Chuck said, "You'll be back." I took that as a promise.

So I went back down to Triple-A and though I felt like a yo-yo, I hit .324 in fifty-six games there and was, as the scouts reported, the best player in the league. I was called up on August 26 for the pennant run. Chuck told me on the phone, "I wanted you to go down there, and you did exactly what I asked you to do. You got yourself ready to play." He wanted me there because Foli was hurt. So I flew from Spokane to Los Angeles,

Dad was born Lorenzo Pietro Berra to Pietro and Paolina Berra. He had three older brothers—Mike, Tony, and John—and a sister, Josie.

Dad's childhood home at 5447 Elizabeth Avenue, Dago Hill, in St. Louis.

Dad in his Naval uniform circa 1944.

Uncle John, Papa
Berra, and Dad.

Papa and Mama Berra with Dad in 1947.

As a player, Dad won an astonishing ten World
Series Championships with the Yankees,
including six with Whitey Ford (center) and
seven with Mickey Mantle (right).

My family down at Spring Training in
St. Petersburg in 1947. I'm the baby.

Arriving at Yankee Stadium in 1959.
I'm ready to hit.

Carmen Short Berra, the love of Dad's
life, my incredible Mom, and the glue
that held our family together.

Hitting in the batting cages at Spring
Training in 1970. I was a teenager, thrilled to
be wearing a real Major League uniform.

With my Dad on the bench at
Wrigley Field in 1970.

Dad's induction into the Baseball Hall of Fame in 1972.

The day I was drafted in June of 1975.

Being fired by the Mets allowed Dad to finally watch me play. Here we are in Niagara Falls in 1975.

I played for the Pittsburgh
Pirates from 1977 to 1984.

My manager Chuck Tanner
congratulates me on a
go-ahead home run in 1983.

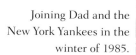

Joining Dad and the
New York Yankees in the
winter of 1985.

A game-winning home run swing in the bottom of the tenth against the Detroit Tigers off of pitcher Guillermo Hernandez on July 1, 1986.

I'm congratulated at home plate by Mike Easler, Dennis Rasmussen, Don Mattingly, Butch Wynegar, and Lou Piniella.

My brothers, Timmy and Larry, and me with my Dad in 2010.

Dad at the Yogi Berra Museum, opened in 1998.

On November 24, 2015, only two months after he left us, Dad was awarded the highest honor a citizen can receive, the Presidential Medal of Freedom.

My daughter, Whitney.

With my wife Jane and our daughters, Alexandra and Kay.

where the Pirates were playing a series against the Dodgers. But when I got in, there was a message to call Harding. He began by saying he was sorry—never a good thing to hear—but he couldn't call me up; as a nonroster player, I had to wait until the minor league season ended. You'd think a GM would know that all along, but evidently they didn't or thought they could get around it.

Five days later, on September 1, I yo-yoed again, flying to San Francisco, where Chuck put me right in the lineup against the Giants in Candlestick Park, batting in the eight hole. I had a big day. In the fifth inning, with us trailing 3-0, I led off with a homer against John "The Count" Montefusco. An inning later, after Pops also took one out, I hit a sacrifice fly to tie it. We went on to win 5-3. At the time, we were in the middle of a six-game winning streak, three and a half games ahead of the Montreal Expos. I played short in twenty of the last thirty games, on a bad ankle, got some key hits, and made only five errors. And we needed every hit and errorless play because the Expos—a hell of a team, with two future Hall of Famers, Gary Carter and Andre Dawson—just wouldn't go away.

They were in first place as late as September 24, when they beat us 7-6 in Three Rivers in the third game of a huge five-game series. But then, in the final week of a death match, we went to work. As the loudspeakers in the stands blared out "We Are Family," we bashed them the next two games, 10-4 and 10-1, to go back into first place. On the last day, against the Cubs, we needed a win to clinch—and got it, 5-3, our ninety-eighth of the season. I couldn't play in those critical games because Tim was healthy again. Even so, Chuck told me flat out, "Dale, without you we don't win the pennant." That was a

113

tremendous rush. And he was right. My job was to not lose the pennant for us because Foli was hurt. And when a man like Chuck Tanner tells you that's just what you did, there's nothing you don't think you can accomplish.

However, the downer was that I was ineligible for the post-season, as are all players who get called up in September. Again, you'd think a manager would know these things, but Chuck had already had me penciled in on the postseason roster until it dawned on him. He said if somebody got hurt I would be put on the roster. But nobody got hurt and the roster was rock solid. That was the last great Pirates team. Everybody hit like hell. Madlock hit .328, Parker .310. Omar Moreno stole seventy-seven bases. We had the best defense, the best relief pitcher, Kent Tekulve. They went on to beat the Baltimore Orioles in the Series, which saw the last great virtuoso performance for Pops. At thirty-nine, he had done the impossible, winning the league's MVP award (actually sharing it with Keith Hernandez), hit .455 in the playoff sweep over the Cincinnati Reds, then .400 in the Series with three homers—including one in game 7, winning the Series MVP as well.

I went with the team to Baltimore for the first two games. Chuck said I could sit in the dugout, in uniform, during the games. But that also ran afoul of the rules. As the commissioner's office put it, almost comically, I could have passed along "secret information" that might influence a game—though to exactly whom I would pass it was unclear. That's a small example of the bull you put up with from the baseball establishment.

So I had to go sit in the stands, freezing my ass off because it was so cold it snowed for the first game. I hated every minute. I'm not a watcher; I'm a player. When the series shifted to Pittsburgh, I told Chuck it was too difficult to watch and not be able to contribute.

I went back home to Montclair and could barely watch it on TV. Dad, who was home in October for the first time in three years, kept telling me to stop feeling sorry for myself. "You can't change things you got no control over," he said. "You did good, you helped them win, be happy with that." Easy for him to say. But he was right, and I cheered myself up knowing I had a future on the team as it would enter a new decade.

I was gratified that my teammates thought enough of my contribution to vote to give me a three-quarters cut of the winner's share, which was $100,000 per player, so I got $75,000. not too shabby considering my salary that year was $30,000. That was a rarity; sometimes those issues about what a part-timer deserves cause fights among the regular players. I had an agent then, a big-time one, Ed Keating, the first real super-agent, who began in the '60s representing Arnold Palmer and had built a stable of players in every sport. In '75, when free agency exploded after an arbitrator lifted the reserve clause in players' contracts that had bound them to their teams, Ed took Gary Matthews from $46,000 a year to a five-year, $1.8 million deal. The power of the players was really on the rise, and with it would come something never seen in my dad's time—labor versus management strife. My contract would jump to $75,000 the next year and soon zoom into the stratosphere. It was hard to believe that I could feel any higher. But that same winter, I learned that I could.

I never used hard drugs up until the early '80s. As a teenager, I'd sneaked a few beers, like all kids, but my drug of choice was baseball. It would always be. But you never know how much circumstances will change you when you get older, especially when you become a key player on a big-league team who's just at the tip of the iceberg of how good you can be, and you're suddenly making big money, and you're only twenty-three. Then, too, ballplayers were a different breed when I came into baseball. As I said, even back when Dad was managing the Mets in the early '70s, guys on that team, guys I idealized, were smoking pot.

Neither Dad nor his coaches had any idea about it. I'm sure Dad would have sent heads rolling if he did. But he had enough to do without babysitting adult men. In the end, we all make our own beds; nobody will be there to keep you from your own devices. When you think about it, Dad had seen an earlier version of the same thing, when he kept Mickey's drinking and carousing secret from the writers. Mickey in spring training was drunk every day. He just never showed it, so you left him alone. He played hungover and still hit balls out of the park.

Those guys from that generation were completely in the dark about hard drugs. Chuck didn't know all the shit that was going on, and there was plenty. That was the era when cocaine scandals began making headlines in pro football, the ugliest rumors about it in Dallas, by Cowboys players like Thomas "Hollywood" Henderson, who would admit to using cocaine on the sideline, *during a Super Bowl.* In '77, Miami Dolphins defensive linemen Randy Crowder and Don Reese were sent to jail for cocaine trafficking. If Tom Landry and Don Shula, two of the most dictatorial coaches of all time, didn't know what was going on with their own players, you knew you could get away with it, unless the law stepped in. And even so, Crowder and Reese were still allowed to play after they got out of jail. As it was, there was sort of a scandal in baseball when Pete Rose said he was doing "greenies," which was what amphetamines were called. They weren't illegal back then, and big-league clubhouses had bowls full of them; guys would scoop a handful of them before going out on the field. I tried them, and they made me want to run through a wall. We didn't know the damaging effects of stimulants on the heart and nervous system, or the addictive nature of it. Cocaine turned up that quotient to the nth degree. It wasn't just addictive and life-threatening. It was also illegal.

However, it wasn't the high life of an athlete or the accessibility of drugs that got me started on cocaine. That happened right in my own hometown, at a time when my generation was experimenting with harder drugs than booze and weed. The fact is, I was late to the party. I'd never done any of the stuff I knew guys around baseball were doing. Someone would pass me a joint at a hotel or someplace, and I'd say no thanks. I wasn't a pot person. I didn't want to be paranoid; I wanted to be euphoric. But then when I got home during the off-season, either '79 or '80, all my old friends were now doing coke. It was like someone turned on a switch and suddenly everyone was sniffing white powder up their noses. In a lot of ways, those guys had more influence on me than a Willie Stargell, because we'd grown up together. You didn't feel like you had to watch what you said and did or like you were in the presence of greatness; you just partied.

I was still living at home, with Mom and Dad. Larry and Timmy were married, on their own, living in homes in the Montclair area, raising families. Obviously, the old streetlight rule was long gone. I'd stay out all night and stumble in at the crack of dawn. By the time I'd get up, I'd be fine. No cause for Mom and Dad to know I was partying like it was 1999. And when I say my old buddies were using, I mean all of them. Every time I went out, guys were going out back and doing it. Every party was inundated with cocaine. Montclair is an upscale community, but money wasn't even the main factor. There was always a mix of rich and not rich. Coke was expensive, but back then someone would have it and share it. We never really knew who had bought it.

The first time for me was like that. It was at a New Year's Eve party. I was drinking, feeling good. I was still on a natural high from what Chuck said about me winning the pennant for him. And when the powder came around, I relented. The times I'd had the chance to do it before, I'd actually been afraid to. It scared me. But I let down my natural guard. I said, oh hell, let me try it. And when it went into my nostrils and got into my brain and nerve endings, I liked the feeling. Liked it too much. Way too much. I'd never felt that way in my life. I was euphoric, on top of the world; the only thing that came close was hitting a home run. And I had to go days, weeks, between those. From then on, I was hooked. A couple weeks later, if I knew there was a party, I got a half a gram from a buddy, and the cycle of using and buying had begun. It made me feel, I don't know, smart. Worldly. Talkative. Knowledgeable. I was in a funhouse, having the time of my life.

I didn't think at the time about why I was so receptive to it, but I've thought about it since, and I believe it had something to do with the fact that I'm obsessive-compulsive. I once read where somebody gave a lecture to the best lawyers in the country and asked how many of them were obsessive-compulsive and 90 percent of them raised their hands. That goes for a lot of successful people. I could see that many athletes are obsessive-compulsive. I probably got it from Dad. It made him better, and it made me better. Whatever I did, I did it to the best of my ability. The effort was always 100 percent. And so you could say I gave 100 percent to doing coke. In the end, it was a personality thing. Something inside me said to do it, to hit it and not quit it.

That makes sense to me. But what I know more than 100 percent is that I didn't do it because of anything in my family. There was no symbolic rebellion from my dad, no reaction to any pressure he put on me. Because there never was any. I never in my life did a drug because I was depressed, because I looked in the mirror and didn't like who I saw, or because I needed it to fit in with shady people. If any shrink in rehab would have ever told me that there was a cavity in my soul, I would have walked out. My family was absolutely perfect. My relationships with my parents were wonderful. There was no deep-seated resentment toward anybody. I was completely happy, never had any void in my life. I just somehow made a very poor choice because, literally, everybody was doing it.

Neither did I push it to excess. At the beginning, I hardly needed any coke. It was new to me, my body, and a little went a long way. I pretty much maintained that routine. I didn't need a lot. I wasn't a greedy user. I was setting up the rationalization that I was just an occasional, recreational user, too smart to get into deep trouble, doing it the "right" way, the "responsible" way. Don't worry, I assured myself, I could control it, not the other way around. I believed it, too. You remember in the movie *The Big Chill* when someone says it's harder going a week without a rationalization than sex? They got that right, brother.

Nobody could have convinced me back then that I would harm myself and my career. It seemed so easy, even natural. When I went to spring training for the '80 season, I had no intention of leaving cocaine behind in New Jersey. It's not like I announced to my Pirates teammates, "Hey, anybody got some blow?" No one would ever do that. You just made yourself open to it when the opportunity arose. For example, many of the players stayed at the Franklin Plaza Hotel downtown. One night, after dinner and a few drinks, I, Dave Parker, John Milner, and Lee Lacy wound up in someone's room. We were just hanging when a guy named Curtis Strong came in. He was a caterer and supplied our clubhouse buffet table, and as a sideline sold coke to players. I'd seen him before but just ignored him. But this time when he went into a side room with some of the guys, I followed along. He asked me what I wanted, and I told him. He then pulled a tin foil package from his pocket. I handed him a hundred-dollar bill and he handed me the coke.

That wasn't the first time I'd scored some coke, or the last. I had other places I could get it, and it got to a point where these kind of deals kept going down, at hotels, even inside the clubhouse. Another guy was named Shelby Greer, a friend of Dave's who sometimes came on road trips with us. We had a very open clubhouse in those days. Anybody could come in. All you had to do was tell the guard to let them in. Somebody always needed something. Not everyone did coke. Pops, for one, never did coke in his life, but he did use greenies; we all did.

It wasn't like we were sneaking around. It wasn't a crack house kind of thing—well, maybe it was for Rod Scurry, who got into freebasing cocaine, the much more dangerous form of the drug that's smoked out of a pipe, which soon became known as crack. Rod took it so much further than the rest of us that we kind of avoided him, but it was hard ignoring a guy who sat at his locker swearing that snakes were crawling up his arms. He'd frantically shake his shoulders to get rid of the imaginary crawlers. We knew something was up with Rod but pretty much left him alone, and he pitched well, so we never thought, "Hey, let's get this dude some help."

Doing cocaine wasn't something we feared. We just got together like ballplayers do, and instead of getting liquored up, we did something else that made us feel good. With my personality, I felt too good. I liked it too much, although I consciously kept it on the lowest level of usage, purely recreational, a little each time. I never gave Chuck a reason to think I wasn't completely professional. I never missed a game, a plane, or a team banquet or engagement. I was ready to play every day. That's how you can tell yourself you're controlling it. When I kept rising on the baseball ladder, I was in high gear, no pun intended. I kept getting better, won a starting job, was playing nearly every game. When I would kick back and use, I felt even better. Looking back, I wasn't just chasing a pennant. I was chasing euphoria.

Unfortunately, winning in '79 would be the Pirates' last crowning moment. Pops would play another couple years but was hurt a lot and replaced as the starting first baseman by Milner, then Jason Thompson. The Phillies would be resurgent, passing us by. We finished third in '80, but, finally free of the minor leagues, I played in ninety-three games, starting sixty-three, splitting time between third and short, and even a little second base. I hit .220, six homers, thirty-one RBIs, still that work in progress but established. The next season, my progression continued—but so did the labor strife. When the two sides couldn't come to an agreement over free agency, the players went out on strike, for the first time during a season. We went on the picket line from June 12 until July 31. Over seven hundred games were canceled, the players lost $4 million a week, and the owners lost $72 million overall. To salvage the season, a crazy split-season format was used to determine playoff teams—but nothing could have gotten us in, that year was a total loss, though I was satisfied raising my average to .241.

The '82 season was my unveiling as a regular. The Pirates had traded Foli to the California Angels, and Chuck told me, "You're gonna play every day." Chuck was a stat guy, and he said that based on my RBIs per at-bat and games, "projected over the season, you're going to be one of the most productive offensive shortstops in the game." If I got six hundred at-bats, the projections were thirty-one homers and seventy RBIs, quite a tall order. Tim had been a great glove man but was an undisciplined hitter who had little power and almost never walked.

In fact, that year for the Angels, he walked only fourteen times, then a record for playing in at least 150 games.

Chuck wanted me to prove his theory about an eighth-place hitter being much more than an easy out. Tim was also a bit of a hothead; when he was a coach on the Reds in 2000, he got into a fight with another coach. Chuck wanted a cooler head and hotter bat. That's not what he got. I was hitting just .180 after the first month and a half and was down. I couldn't catch a break. Once, I came up with the bases loaded, two outs in the ninth, and hit one of the hardest shots of my life, right up the middle, a sure gamer. But it just nicked the pitcher's leg and ricocheted to the shortstop, who threw me out. But Chuck kept slapping me on the back and saying, "Pick your head up, kid, you're in the big leagues."

"Skip," I said, "I'm just not doing well."

"Listen," he said, "you can strike out three times with the bases loaded or make a bad error, but there aren't many guys in the world who can lose a major league baseball game. You're good enough to be in a position to do that."

Now *that's* optimism.

He stuck with me, because he believed in me. And, sure enough, by the All-Star break I was hitting .270, driving in runs, hitting home runs, the whole schmear. I wound up playing all but six games, with 529 at-bats, hitting .263. I didn't come near thirty homers, but my ten dingers tied me among National League shortstops with Atlanta's Rafael Ramírez and helped me drive in sixty-one runs—from the number 8 hole, mind you—right in line with the projection. I also was fourth in total bases among the league shortstops. And, fulfilling

Chuck's goal, I was intentionally walked nine times, and thirty-three times in all, to get to the pitcher. I was on a good roll, more comfortable, able to stay in a groove.

The other players noticed. Mike Schmidt came up to me during a game with the Phillies and said, "Kid, you're the best eight hitter in this league." Pete Rose echoed that. When I couldn't get a hit, he patted me on the ass when we played the Reds and said, "Don't worry, you play this game the right way." And Schmidt wasn't even a particularly nice guy, especially toward opposing players. Pete was different. You'd get to first base and he'd say, "How's your old man doing, kid? Good. Tell him I said hello." Then you'd get to second and Larry Bowa is out there and he'd say, "How you doin', kid? How's Dad?" But then you'd get to third and Schmidt glared at you, his red eyebrows narrowing. It was all business. You were the enemy. So for him to praise me like that was rare. Made me feel ten feet tall.

Hitting was only half my game. The other half was defense. And I thought Chuck's verdict on that was obvious when he said in spring training the next year that Johnny Ray and I were the most productive shortstop/second-base combination in the league. He was mainly speaking about our offensive stats, but Johnny and I had to be dependable as all-around players or else lose those starting jobs. Yeah, I did make some errors, thirty in all, but I had excellent range: I could go get a grounder in the hole and throw a guy out, or cross over to the second-base side of the infield to snare a sure hit. My arm was strong, but erratic. I played the game balls to the wall, with a lot of confidence. Maybe I should have put some of those grounders in my back pocket instead of throwing to first.

The fans at Three Rivers were very good to me, right from the start, and I loved them. But some began getting on me for the errors. And that was picked up and magnified even more by the sportswriters. I began to see myself in the papers being called "Boo Boo"—after Yogi Bear's cartoon buddy. That was unfair, since my fielding percentage was actually .961, not Ozzie Smith or Chris Speier territory, but only a few points behind Larry Bowa. The year before, Foli's percentage was .965, and he was never called Boo Boo.

When analytics came into vogue in baseball, a new statistic was created, wins above replacement, or WAR, which calculates how many wins a guy contributed to above a replacement-level player. Retroactively applying it to the past, it was determined that I ranked fourth in the National League that season in defensive WAR. Turns out I accounted for 2.4 wins above replacements. The only National Leaguers who had a higher defensive WAR were Ozzie Smith, Gary Carter—both Hall of Famers—and Dickie Thon, a great defensive shortstop. (Here's another anomaly—I was no speed merchant, but in '81 I led the league in stolen-base percentage, eleven out of twelve, or 91.67, beating out Davey Lopes and my teammate Lee Lacy.)

I had to live with that Boo Boo stigma for another year or so before it kind of faded away. I only made as many as thirty errors in a season once more, and my overall career WAR is 5.5, meaning I was responsible for five wins more than all others who replaced me. To be honest, the slights meant little to me. What mattered was being able to help the team. We couldn't have played any harder that '82 season. Madlock hit .319, Tony Peña .296, Thompson .284. Parker was still dangerous. Johnny

Ray, in his first full year, played every game at second and hit well. Tony Peña was a rock at catcher. John Candelaria's ERA was under 3.00. Pops, in his last year, could still go up there once in a while and deliver a huge hit, and always leadership. Tekulve was thirty-five but king of the pen. But once the calendar turned to September, we couldn't put it together and finished fourth at 84-78, eight games behind the eventual champion St. Louis Cardinals.

Still, I was feeling great. Maybe a little too great, for reasons that had nothing to do with baseball.

CHAPTER 6

Eight Miles High

EVEN AFTER I became established, to a lot of media people I was still Yogi's boy. Often when a story was written about me, that was the angle. In '82, a reporter heard me ask Bill Madlock when he came in the clubhouse if it was raining. When he said it was, I asked, "Wet rain or dry rain?" That, wrote the reporter, "certainly seem[ed] to qualify [Dale] as a definitive chip off the old block." Yes, it did sound like a Yogi-ism—I was pretty good at giving my own versions, in jest, because people kind of expected me to, such as when Harding Peterson asked me how I compared myself to Dad. "Basically," I said, "our similarities are different." Harding sort of blinked. Then, a few minutes later, he came back. "Did you say what I think you said?"

I never minded giving the writers what they wanted to write that same "chip off the old block" story, over and over again. As long as I was getting my due as a player. There were a few other sons of famous players who'd made the big leagues with me, such as Bump Wills, Bob Boone, Buddy Bell, Roy Smalley—and, of course, Cal Ripken Jr., who would win a championship in his second full season with the Baltimore Orioles in 1983. We all earned our place. We all shared the pride of our birth-rights and the pride we had in ourselves. And Dad was still there for me, at a distance. During the season, he would call me a lot—even from the dugout, during a game. Our game would end before the Yankees game, and he'd call our club-house between innings. Don't ask me how he knew the num-ber, he just did; he had all kinds of little inside information like that. Our trainer would pick up and call to me, "Hey, kid, your old man's on the phone."

The first time he did that I said, "What do you mean he's on the phone? The Yankees are playing right now, for Christ's sake." Sometimes I wish he hadn't called. Because he'd say something like, "What the hell, Dale. You struck out three times tonight?"

"How do you know that?"

"I got the box score."

"Dad, Sutton's hard."

"He's gotta throw it over the plate, don't he? Hell, I didn't strike out three times in a month."

He always thought it was fair to compare himself to mere mortals. I'd laugh at it. "Dad, Christ almighty, you're a different animal. Nobody can hit like you."

He never knew why that was. If he could do things, he couldn't understand why everyone else couldn't. I mentioned before that he never thought he was in a slump; he just wasn't getting hits. He told me, "I went zero-for-thirty-five once when I was going bad," which is hard to believe. "What did you do?" I asked. He said, "I didn't do nothin'. I was hitting it good, so I knew they'd be droppin' in soon, and they did."

In general, though, he still wanted to keep that buffer zone between us. We would talk a lot, mainly about pitchers I was about to face and so on. I'd say, "I got Andújar tonight," and he'd have a little scouting report on him, inside his head. These conversations were important, but to me the most important thing about them was how they ended, with our standard dialogue. Him asking me if I was all right, me saying I was, and then him saying what I always waited for.

"Kid, that's all I wanna hear."

The '83 season was a replay of '82. We were at or near the top of the National League East all season. We began September tied with the Phillies, and the Cardinals and Expos were just behind us. We had a six-game winning streak midmonth that kept us up there, but then lost three of four, fell out of first, and when we lost four of our last five, that was all she wrote. We finished second, six games behind the Phillies, with the same record as the year before, 84-78. I played all but one game—Mr. Iron Man, if only for one season—hit .251 with ten homers and fifty-two RBIs. That was the season I led the league in intentional walks, nineteen of them, batting in that number 8 hole. For trivia freaks, that was two more than Mike Schmidt, the Hall of Famer Mike Schmidt, who hit thirty-five homers and walked a league-high 107 times. Remember this. I had fifty-two RBIs even while getting walked nineteen times intentionally, meaning those were situations when I would have had the chance to drive men in or they wouldn't have bothered walking me. I would have had the chance to have a lot more

RBIs. Teams knew I'd led the league shortstops in RBIs the year before, they knew not to pitch to me. I had sixty-one walks in all. Hitting eighth.

I also led the major leagues in catcher's interference, when their mitts would make contact with my bat or get in my way when I hit the ball. Why that was I don't really know; it just seemed a coincidence, but a record's a record, right? Chuck even asked me once in San Francisco if I could get an interference on purpose. I said, "No, Skip, I can't." Still improving, doing my thing on and off the field. I'd go back to the hotel, maybe do some coke, and not touch it for a week afterward. It all seemed very natural. I wasn't bothering anyone, causing a disturbance, making any trouble for myself. You couldn't have guessed I was using coke because I was hyper to begin with, and coke never really altered my outward behavior because I didn't do all that much at a time. Again, the "right" way to do it.

After the season, I returned to Montclair. My brothers and I have always lived within a mile or so of each other, in and around Montclair. I always kept in shape during the off-season, and in '84, I anticipated a real breakout season. So did the Pirates, because they gave me and Johnny Ray five-year contracts to lock both of us up. My deal was for $1.5 million, a real vote of confidence. However, that was when the worm began to turn. For the first time, I had to deal with an injury. In late August, I developed bursitis in my elbow and it became infected. My right arm blew up twice its size, and I had to go on the disabled list for something like fifteen games. During that period of inactivity, I put on a few pounds, which didn't help, and my arm was never really right. The thirty errors I made that season were a product of that. I still played 136 games, meaning that other than the time I spent on the DL, I was almost always in there. But my numbers fell—.222, nine homers, fifty-two RBIs. My intentional walks dropped to eight.

I was struggling. We started off bad and got worse, mired in last place from April 25 on. We ended 75-87, an incredible twenty-one and a half games behind. But when you're fortunate enough to put a big-league uniform on and play a kid's game for a living, even when you're out of it you have to try to play the game with the same passion as if you're in a pennant race. You'd still rather be there than any other place in the world. It was my job to get out there and play. But it was never just a job. There was always something to play for. You go as hard as you can. It's the same feeling you have when you're in Little League. But everybody is judged on their numbers. What Chuck had said about me and Johnny was true, and Johnny didn't let him down. He hit .312 that year, leading the league with thirty-eight doubles for the second straight year and playing his position almost flawlessly. But I didn't hold up my end. That was the year I should have taken off, but I went in reverse.

As a team, we all did. Only five years after the hysteria all around us, we were a last-place team. The pitching was still good, but Pops was gone and Parker and Moreno were traded, Omar to the Yankees. Guys like Marvell Wynne and Doug Frobel were in the outfield, and nobody hit more than seventeen homers. The fans had grown impatient. That is, the fans who came to the park, which for some games looked like a sea of empty seats. We all were showered with boos at some point, and I got a good share of the abuse. And you know what? I couldn't blame them. I was a big New York Giants football fan, and I used to boo Phil Simms like everybody else when he threw interceptions. The fact was, I had shown a lot of potential, and realized some of it, but while I was still productive, I was underachieving. Looking back, I know why, although I refused to see it then.

The first sign that something was going south was my reflexes. I saw the ball as well, I wasn't slower, but my reaction time ticked down. That doesn't happen when you're twenty-eight unless you're doing something to affect that part of your brain. If I had known that it was the coke, I would have stopped immediately—or at least I hope I would have. I may have been too stupid to stop, anyway. Instead, I passed it off as just a bad year. After all, I felt good. I wasn't overdoing coke. I didn't miss games. I didn't miss workouts. I was always there, on time. I didn't need to use coke in the morning to get myself rolling, didn't ever do it before a game. I never got into the more potent and dangerous forms of using coke, freebasing or injecting it. I was deathly afraid of that, and I never saw anyone ever doing it that way. I was a moderate user.

What I was fooling myself about was the cumulative effect. Cocaine will eat into your brain, your systems, your reactions. All of them will slow down. The insidious thing is that it takes time for that to happen, so you have to look for warning signs. I wasn't looking. But even though I kept telling Dad I was all right, I wasn't. What he didn't know—because I didn't know— was that I was sabotaging my career and my life, and dirtying the surname I wore so proudly on my back. And now, as fate would have it, I was going to be a lot closer to him. Like right there in the same dugout.

Fate does work in mysterious ways. After the Yankees won ninety-one games but finished third in '83, George Steinbrenner had fired Billy Martin for the third time (though he officially remained with the team as an adviser). A day later, December 17, Dad signed a two-year contract at age fifty-eight to manage for a second time the team he had given most of his life to. The move was met with delight all throughout New York and among the players. Dad, as always, was cool about it, saying he hadn't asked for the job and that they didn't have far to go to win it all. But after spending eight years as a Yankees coach, I could see he was excited about being the main man again, and the family was overjoyed for him.

If George hired him to be a name on a marquee and take orders from above, he found out Yogi Berra was no puppet. He had his own ideas and made some changes right away. The Yankees were an old team and he wanted to go with young guys he believed in. The best of them was Don Mattingly, who like me had started in pro ball at age eighteen, torn up the minors for four years, and made the big club in '83, hitting .283 in ninety-one games, splitting first base with the aging Ken Griffey Sr. Dad also wanted to ease in a replacement at third base for thirty-eight-year-old Graig Nettles, as great a glove man as there ever was but in decline. Dad traded for veteran Toby Harrah, and then dealt Nettles to the San Diego Padres, but he had his eye on Mike Pagliarulo, who like Donnie was only twenty-three and started the season in Triple-A. Dave Righetti, just twenty-five, had won fourteen games as a starter in '83. Dad moved him into the bullpen, as the closer.

Dad was thrilled to have great veterans like Dave Winfield in the outfield, Don Baylor at DH, Willie Randolph at second, and my old teammate Omar Moreno in center. But he wanted the young guys—his guys, he called them, channeling Casey Stengel—to take over and didn't want to wait. When the Detroit Tigers got off to a ridiculous 32-5 start and the Yankees were ten games behind at the end of April with an 8-13 record, he said, "I'm playing my guys." Griffey went to center field so Mattingly could play every day. Roy Smalley was replaced at shortstop with Bobby Meacham, who was also twenty-three and in his first full season. In July, Pagliarulo was called up.

All this activity didn't pay off right away. On July 3, the team was a staggering twenty-one games behind, still nine games under .500. George, imploding with every loss, called Dad into his office—never a good thing. He didn't fire Dad, which might have been suicidal, but he did all but order him to play the veteran guys Dad had moved out. George seemed particularly miffed about the kids at the corners and lobbied for Steve Kemp to play first base, and Smalley third. Dad listened, sat up straight, and threw down the gauntlet.

"I'm playing Mattingly at first and I'm playing Pags at third," he said. "And if you don't like it"—now he picked up a pack of matches and threw it across the desk—"fucking fire me." Then he strode out of the room.

It's doubtful anyone had ever spoken like that to George, who always lived up—or down—to his moniker of "the Boss." He must not have known what to say—another first. But as

Dad walked out, he knew he was beaten. Dad was not going to take orders. It had been a long time since D-Day.

If the team had continued to play badly, I'm sure Dad would have been fired. But they didn't. They caught fire, going 54-34 the last three months, finishing in third place but with an 87-75 record. Mattingly ended up winning the batting title at .343 and came in fifth in the MVP race. Ask Donnie about that season and he will tell you not that he did these things but that Dad fought for him. I think every Yankee felt the same. Dad came home for the winter satisfied he hadn't let them quit and had stood up to George and lived to tell the tale. And that's when our professional paths merged.

In Pittsburgh, Chuck and Harding were working toward remaking the Pirates. After their disastrous season, suddenly keeping me and Johnny Ray together wasn't so important. That's how suddenly things can turn in baseball. I knew I was on the trading block and had no objection to that. Sometimes you just need a change of scenery to get your edge back. I had no idea if the Yankees were interested in me. Dad said he thought I could help them at third base, where Mike Pagliarulo was penciled in but was only in his second year, having played just sixty-seven games as a rookie. But Dad played it coy. The only thing he told me was that "things could be in the works." You bet he was a really good poker player.

It didn't take long for the new Yankee GM, Clyde King, to make the decision. On December 20, 1984, just three days after Dad agreed to manage in 1985 with the assurance from Steinbrenner that he would not be fired, the Pirates traded me along with pitcher Alfonso Pulido and minor league outfielder Jay Buhner to the Yankees for Steve Kemp, Tim Foli—who would bounce back to Pittsburgh—and cash, which the Yankees had a lot of. The next day, we drove together to Yankee Stadium for a press conference, both of us wearing suits and Yankee caps. We smiled a lot and hugged for the cameras, one of the greatest moments of my life. Many made the assumption that Dad had pulled the strings to get me. And he did make it known he wanted me, but not for personal reasons. He needed depth at third base, and I had the credentials. Dad being Dad, he told it like it was.

"At the ballpark, he's just another player to me. If he can play, he plays. If he doesn't, he sits."

That off-season was going to be a happy one in any case. I'd bought a home in Glen Ridge, around five minutes from Dad's house and my brothers' and began what should have been a joyous winter. And I would move into it as a married man. I'd been going with a local girl from Montclair named Leigh O'Grady, a fun Irish gal I'd met when I was home for an off-season and she was a senior in high school. We set a date for after the new year, which began with me on a natural high.

My sense of excitement was obvious when I told the press, and meant it, "Fortunately, I didn't get traded to Cleveland." I wasn't lying when I said the Yankees were the team I always wanted to play for, and while it probably would be easier on Dad if he was a coach rather than manager, there would only be pressure on me if I messed up. "If I play well," I added, "the possibilities are endless."

Dad kept on playing it cool, but Whitey Ford, who knew

him so well, told the press, "Yogi's tickled about it." That made two of us. But even Whitey cautioned that if I made mistakes, "Yogi'll chew his butt good." I knew that, too. Because he kept telling me all winter.

I truly believed I would bring the Yankees more intensity. As I pointed out, "I'm hyper on the field, very talkative, in constant motion"—which was natural, not a product of cocaine. "I don't know where I get that," I said. "My dad was quiet. And his little short dumpy body could hit better than my 'good' body. I don't have that intuitive thing going for me that he did. When I'm going good, I flow. You make plays you don't think you can make. But sometimes I think too much and try too hard."

That was pretty honest talk, but that was just me. I'm my own toughest critic. In some ways, I played like Pete Rose, taking it to the limit every play. All I ever asked for was a chance to prove myself. So did Dad.

But, in the blink of an eye, the winter got a lot colder. In early January, the doorbell rang at my mom and dad's house at six a.m. I didn't know it, but that was the beginning of a whole new turn in my life. I still hadn't moved into the house in Glen Ridge, so I was upstairs sleeping in my old room, just as I always had after baseball season ended. Mom and Dad were sleeping in their own room, and Mom got up and answered the door. A few minutes later, half-asleep, I saw her come into my room, looking a little ashen.

"There are two men downstairs who want to talk to you," she said. "They say they're from the FBI."

I didn't know what to say. To be honest, this wasn't a complete shock to me. There had been some talk going around the league toward the end of the season that there was an investigation of some sort about drug dealers in baseball. But I comforted myself with the assumption—the wrong assumption—that they would not bother with me, a small fry. It was the same old song. But it was the wrong song.

When I got downstairs, the FBI guys told me that they had a subpoena for me to appear in front of a federal grand jury in Pittsburgh investigating drug trafficking in the city. They were respectful and polite, and didn't treat me like I was some sort of criminal, because I wasn't. I was in no danger of prosecution for anything I did. But that's all they would tell me. They were only there to serve the subpoena, then they were back out the door.

Mom and Dad had left me alone with them, giving me privacy. After the guys left, both of them came down and asked what it was all about. I explained that they just wanted me to testify about drug use in Pittsburgh but that I wasn't involved in anything bad, that I was just a witness, which I was.

But you could never pull the wool over Dad's eyes. He was too smart.

"Is this about you?" he asked. "Are you in trouble?"

"No, Dad, I just have to tell the truth about what I know."

That was the first time I ever had to walk a tightrope about drugs with my parents. Not that I was in fact some sort of criminal, but it was not fun to have to tell your folks you had used drugs. I said it had been just a recreational thing, not an addiction, told them not to worry.

"Are you all right?" Dad asked. "That's all I wanna know."

"Yes, Dad. I'm fine."

A couple weeks later, I went and testified. Only then did I find out the scope of the investigation. I was one of eleven players known to have purchased cocaine, mainly current and ex-Pirates including Rod Scurry, Dave Parker, Lee Lacy, John Milner, Al Holland, Lee Mazzilli, and other stars like Keith Hernandez, Tim Raines, Lonnie Smith, Jeffrey Leonard, and Enos Cabell. The first to be identified was Scurry, the pitcher who had come up with me and had missed a month of the '84 season undergoing cocaine rehabilitation. But security was so tight when I entered the courthouse—the entire ninth floor was sealed off to the media—that no one knew which players had been called to testify. There were rumors that Willie Stargell testified, but he never was called. The questions and answers were over and done in a few hours, and I was on my way home. All I did was tell the truth about cocaine use on the Pirates, that I'd used it a few times and that I'd bought from Curtis Strong. Moreover, in order to get to the real targets, the dealers like Strong, all of us were granted immunity from prosecution. That was all well and good, but Mom, Dad, and my brothers were shocked and worried about me. I knew they would be.

LARRY: I didn't know he was in any way involved with drugs. It was a complete shock. Mom called and told me what had happened with the FBI the next day, and I said, "Oh my God." I could hear in her voice that she was scared to death. So was Dad. None of us knew what to think.

TIM: I was shocked because we were so close. We didn't spend that much time after we all were married and Dale was playing ball. But I would never even have thought that he would do anything that could ruin his career. Drugs? Shit, that didn't even dawn on me. We were all clean-nosed kids, and Dale was the one who was the most regimented, the levelheaded one who played sports twenty hours a day.

But the culture of the time was everybody did all that crap. Dale was a rambunctious type of guy and sort of an addictive personality, but he's also right that there were no hidden skeletons in our closet he was escaping. I was the rebel, but not against Dad; I just liked being adventurous, not self-destructive. For Dale to do that, I can't even explain it on any rational level.

The newspapers were on the story, with headlines such as SCURRY, BERRA TESTIFY IN GRAND JURY PROBE. And, truthfully, I thought I might be given a much worse third-degree grilling by my own family than I'd gotten by the district attorney. Instead, to my relief, they were totally sympathetic. They didn't confront me; they didn't even know the extent of what I'd done. Dad kept asking the same thing—"Are you all right?" That's all he cared about, was I all right. He didn't say it, but I remembered what he'd told me: don't drag my name into something stupid. I didn't think I would again, or even admit to myself I'd done it now.

LARRY: We didn't confront him. He was a grown man, he was getting married, he had responsibilities. All we could really say was, "I hope you learned your lesson. You're smarter than that." But mostly we worried about his well-being, his health. Dale said don't worry, he didn't have a drug problem, it was a dumb mistake, a recreational thing, it was over. We didn't know how involved he was, and to tell you the truth we didn't want to know.

You'd think I *would* have learned from it; that I would have told myself, okay, even if nothing happens here, you have to be really careful now or risk everything; if you're caught again it's over for you, stop doing coke and stop being stupid. But I had no intention of stopping. It wasn't that I wanted to flout the law; it was just too easy to keep on with my routine, which I always told myself wasn't hurting anyone, not even me. It wasn't like I was trafficking cocaine, selling it, something like that. I was just a guy who did a toot every now and then. Nobody was killing me for doing that, because so many players were doing the same.

It was hard to see the downside of it. I felt I was home free. The wedding went on as scheduled, with not a soul even thinking about the Pittsburgh thing. Timmy was my best man. You would think Dad would be like the Godfather on his daughter's wedding day, that everyone would come over and pay homage to him, he'd be the center of attention. Being Yogi, he couldn't help some of that. And, also being Yogi, there'd be other great Yankees who'd attend with an envelope for you. Whitey, Scooter, Ellie, Gil McDougald, they'd be mingling with everyone. But Dad didn't call attention to himself. He'd hold court at times, tell his stories, but he'd usually blend in, be inconspicuous. He got up and did the spotlight dance with Mom, only because he had to, but no one would have ever seen Yogi Berra dance the tarantella—although I'm sure that with his graceful moves, he would have killed out there. And, no, he didn't call up Sinatra to sing at the wedding.

After I was married and we moved to our new home, I turned my attention totally on my new career as a Yankee. And nobody in the Yankees front office said a thing about the drug issue when I went to spring training, when being managed by my dad was the only story anybody cared about. It wasn't that it was glossed over, or covered up, it just seemed so irrelevant, so small. Not even the writers brought up the grand jury. *Sports Illustrated* didn't even get around to it until late May when it got out that the probe was widening and that there would be grand juries in St. Louis and Atlanta, as well. The magazine reported that there was "evidence of players buying cocaine from dealers in three Pittsburgh bars, in hotel rooms on road trips, and in the parking lot of Three Rivers Stadium. The money laid out for drugs was often substantial—tens of thousands of dollars a year in the case of some players."

Yet, at the same time, it added, "some of the speculation about the Pittsburgh investigation is overblown. Most of the players who testified in Pittsburgh have admitted using cocaine, and it's always possible that some will be indicted. But the targets of the investigation were suppliers, not users...."

None of the guys on the team, or on other teams, mentioned it. I didn't have to make a public apology. The commissioner's office said they'd look into the growing coke problem in baseball, but no action had been taken against us. As far as I was concerned, I was still living a fable. Or maybe in a bubble.

❖❖❖❖

The Yankees' spring training complex in Ft. Lauderdale was the very grounds where Dad had trained in the early '60s, where Mantle and Maris tuned up before their historic dual chase of the Babe's home run record in '61. Of course, anyone just seeing Dad would be transported back in time. He was the same guy, just older. He walked the same, talked the same, put a chaw of tobacco in his mouth the same. And he was always the story. The year before, when he had been hired, *Sports Illustrated* in its baseball preview issue made Dad the central story of the season. They posed him on the cover, back to the camera, the number 8 enough of an identification, gazing out across the field next to the words YOGI'S BACK!

We both enjoyed the hubbub about being the first father and son tandem since Connie and Earle Mack. The first day, Dad teased the reporters, whose numbers dwarfed the press corps in Pittsburgh, and then threw his arm around my shoulder as we, wrote one reporter, "ran up the tunnel to the clubhouse like a couple of happy kids." The vibe around the team was unusually harmonious, which is also something that never changed around Dad. After years of "Bronx Zoo" turmoil, controversy seemed past tense. Even George Steinbrenner seemed pleased. As one article noted, "Each spring the Yankees lead the league in soap opera and locker-room turmoil. This year—with Boss Steinbrenner lying low—everyone in camp is laughing, smiling, kissy-face. The sportswriters are deeply depressed." Sarcasm abounded, one thought being that the real Yankees were kidnapped and on their way to Jupiter. Some wondered if we were the Stepford Yankees.

However, maybe it was an omen when, after we lost a few exhibition games, George was already bitching. "Yogi's not in trouble," he insisted. "I'm willing to take his say-so, but we're getting close [to the season] now and I'm going to have to have some answers soon." With George, there was always a *but*. As one of the writers mused, "The regular season record is 0-0 and [Yogi] already needs a vote of confidence." And, "An intelligent man like Yogi may soon be having second thoughts about this job. He should have learned from watching Billy Martin nearly lose his mind. The only difference between Martin and Berra is that Yogi doesn't deserve this kind of treatment."

Talk about prophetic.

Although most media people thought all the good vibes were as temporary as George would render them, Dad honestly believed the team was primed for a championship. Which was why he had insisted that George give him a verbal promise he would not fire him and allow him to serve out his two-year contract, no matter what. That was for his self-protection, and George's, given that the players would be furious if he fired Dad. That was the big difference between Dad and Billy. Few players ever cried when Billy got fired. It was pointed out that George had made the same promise to Bob Lemon in '78, only to fire Lemon in '82 after fourteen games and hire Gene "Stick" Michael, whom he had fired to hire Lemon. But George asserted, "I put a lot of pressure on my managers in the past...This will not be the case this spring." And Dad, his better angels guiding him as always, believed him.

Dad was serious about changing things. He put us through a flexibility and stretching program. And he also signed off on more bold moves, none bolder than trading five players to the Oakland A's for Rickey Henderson, the best all-around player in the game, who as the quintessential leadoff hitter had hit over .300 twice and stole over one hundred bases three times, setting the Major League record with 130. Henderson was fun to watch, the way he took off on a steal and "snatched" fly balls in center field like a Venus fly trap. He was a real character who often spoke of himself in the third person and made statements like "If you look at some of the people in the Hall of Fame, my numbers are compatible," and "Rickey don't like it when Rickey can't find Rickey's limo." Drawing a dubious parallel, *Sports Illustrated* said he "existed somewhere between fact and fiction," and in this way, "Rickey is the modern-day Yogi Berra, only faster." They could have added less lovable, more self-centered, and less loyal. Dad played his whole career with one team; Rickey played with eleven.

Don't get me wrong. Rickey was a surefire Hall of Famer, and his acquisition reflected Dad's plan for building teams, which he learned from Casey—being strong up the middle: catcher, shortstop, second base, and center field. Rickey, who signed for five years and $8.6 million, seemed to be the last piece of a championship puzzle. Another new piece was a third baseman named Berra, who may have been just another third baseman for his father's team but couldn't help but feel a tickle go down his back when his dad let his guard down for just a minute after being asked during an interview if he was excited about the coming season.

"Yeah," he said, "I'm excited. I'll finally get to see my son play."

CHAPTER 7

A Bronx Jeer and
a Snowstorm in Pittsburgh

THERE WERE SOME protocols we had to get straight. I thought all winter about how to keep a professional distance from Dad, how direct I should be, what I should call him. Skip? Mr. Berra? Yogi? The first day of spring training, when Dad called a team meeting, I had a question for him. I'd decided I would address him the same way I would any other manager, the way I had Chuck. So I began, "Skip"—and before I could get another word out of my mouth, Ron Guidry stood up and interrupted.

"Let's get something straight here now," he drawled in his Cajun accent. "That's your dad; he ain't Skip to you. Don't ever call that man Skip again. You call him Dad, 'cause that's who he is to you."

Just like that, the awkwardness of having your father be your manager evaporated. Gator settled the issue, as he always did, emphatically. He wasn't just a fabulous pitcher; he was the team leader, and nobody would mess with him. From then on,

I called him Dad. I don't know if Earle Mack did that with Connie, but I did, and it was perfectly natural. No one thought that by doing so, I'd get special treatment. Dad wouldn't have allowed that, in any case. To him, I was "kid," same as at home.

It was plenty good enough for me that Dad wanted me to platoon at third with Mike Pagliarulo, playing him against righties, me against lefties, setting up an "Italian hot corner." Pags looked a lot like me with his mustache and dark features, and we were both similar hitters, not high average guys but who could drive in the big run and hit for power on occasion. Pags had more wattage than I did—later in his career he'd hit thirty-two homers in '87, but not more than nine in any season after that. He also had the sort of erratic arm that plagued me from time to time. So we were close and rooted for each other.

We weren't at full strength when the season began. Mattingly, Henderson, and Winfield had nagging injuries that would keep them out of the lineup much of April. When we began against the Boston Red Sox in Fenway Park, Pags played because they started a right-hander. We lost 9-2, Phil Niekro giving up two early homers. I started the second game, jogging to third base, the number 2 on my back (later worn, of course, by none other than Derek Jeter, and in days of yore, Frank Crosetti, the "Old Cro," as Scooter called him, who had played and coached the team for like thirty years, patting guys on the rump when they hit a homer and came around third base). I hit seventh and went two-for-four, though Ed Whitson was also roughed up early, we were behind 9-1 after two innings, and lost 14-5. Then, with Pags back in, we were swept, losing 6-4. This wasn't how things were supposed to go, and we promptly straightened out, sweeping a two-game series in

Cleveland. Gator won the first, and I started both games, going one-for-four in each. We then had our home opener against the Chicago White Sox, before a noisy crowd of over 53,000 fans at Yankee Stadium. I got the nod in that one, too, going zero-for-four, but we won our third in a row, 5-4 on Don Baylor's walk-off homer in the bottom of the ninth.

No use of cocaine can produce a rush like that, and the next game was almost as good. Again I started and, in my first at-bat, drove in the first run on a bloop single off Floyd Bannister. But in the fourth, I made not one but two errors on one play, bobbling a grounder and then throwing wildly past first to let two runs score. It was 2-2 in the bottom of the seventh when Ken Griffey drove in Mattingly with the lead run on a bad-hop single. Dave Righetti, trying for a five-out save, had two runners on, one out, in the ninth. The White Sox tried a double steal. Our catcher, Butch Wynegar, pegged it to me, but Carlton Fisk, the lead runner, had stopped in his tracks and raced back to second. That left the runner at first, Ron Kittle, hung out to dry, halfway to second. Seeing him, I quickly threw to first and we got him out in a rundown. Rags then got the last out.

That put our record at 4-3. And I went two-for-three the next game against the Indians. But in baseball things can go south quick. We lost that one, 2-1, and then Pags got two hits and three RBIs in a 5-2 win. He and I then continued to platoon against righties and lefties, and both of us were hitting well, but the team went into a funk, losing four out of five games—three of them by a single run, one of those in eleven innings, and another by two runs. A hit here, a break there, and we could have been 7-4. And in the final game of the home stand, we beat the Red Sox 5-1. So it's April 25 and we're 6-7, two games out. No, we weren't playing up to our level of talent; we also had nineteen errors. But no one's panicking. I'm hitting .367. And off we flew to Chicago.

Dad was his usual Alfred E. Neuman self: What, me worry? He'd been in the game long enough to know that thirteen games is not a fair barometer of a season—hell, he had come back from much further behind in *August* to win the pennant, twice. He knew we were a good team. He knew that, over the long season, patience isn't a choice; it's a requirement. Needless to say, though, nobody ever called George Steinbrenner a patient man, or an honest one. George was getting all worked up, setting up in his mind justifications to go back on his promise to leave Dad alone. As long as Dad won, he had George over a barrel. Now, George had an opening to make a move, which would close when the team would likely recover.

Not by coincidence, the papers were full of rumors fueled by George that Dad was "in trouble." For the public, George blustered about a "lack of discipline" among the players and a "lack of control of the team" by Dad, both of which were a load of bull. The reality, however, went deeper. I'm sure he'd been steaming for a year about Dad's tongue-lashing, matchbook-throwing episode overruling his orders to play the veterans. There was also the reality that, across town, the Mets had rebuilt into a contender, acquiring Gary Carter, Keith Hernandez, and Ray Knight to go along with Darryl Strawberry and Doc Gooden. They had a holler guy manager, Davey Johnson, and were playing with a lot of hustle and excitement.

We could be just as exciting; we had Rickey, Mattingly, Winfield, and Gator. Maybe Dad wasn't a cheerleader, but we had plenty of pride. And time. As Donnie said, "Geez, I thought maybe we were ten games back. What's the magic number, anyway? Let us alone and let us play." Butch Wynegar, who had signed with us as a free agent in '83 because he dreamed of being coached by Dad, was grim. "You don't see [George] coming out and saying something good. It seems he is always looking for something negative to talk about. It's sad." Said Winfield: "All the guys respect [Yogi], all the guys like him. He's done his job. But you know how they play games around here. And they're playing another one." By "they," he meant only one person.

It also didn't go over well that George was dropping hints about bringing back Billy Martin. An anonymous veteran Yankee was quoted as saying, "We're fed up. Everybody likes and respects Yogi. The other guy . . . well, when we lose, Yogi doesn't hide in his office. He stays at the door of the clubhouse and pats us on the back."

You could feel the angst building. One reporter wrote that, inside our clubhouse, "there is an air of sadness mixed with some anger and bewilderment." Righetti, hopefully, wondered if George was floating the rumors to create "some extra spark to keep Yogi around." But it felt like George was creating a self-fulfilling prophesy, part of which was to condition the team to expect the ax would fall at any minute.

When we landed in Chicago to begin a road trip on Friday night, April 26, there was anything but a spark in our play. Tom Seaver—who made me wince seeing him in his White

Sox uniform, it being my belief that the Mets trading him was the crime of the century—won his 290th career game, beating us 4-2. We didn't help ourselves any leaving fourteen runners on base. (Rickey, back in the lineup for two games, stranded eleven all by himself.) The next two days were worse—the Lost Weekend, to borrow from a famous old movie.

On Saturday, we led 3-1 in the bottom of the ninth. The Sox put two men on against Rags, who struck out the next hitter but then allowed a single and a double that drove in the tying runs. In the top of the eleventh, Rickey worked out a two-out, bases-loaded walk, putting us up 4-3. Bob Shirley came in to save it but, incredibly, he gave up five consecutive singles, the last bringing home the winning run for Chicago. Those were just brutal losses, two of the worst I've ever been in. If we'd been blown out, it might have been better. And then on Sunday, it was—I'll say it—déjà vu all over again. This time, we led 3-1 in the seventh, but Oscar Gamble hit a two-run homer off Joe Cowley to tie it. Then in the bottom of the ninth, with Rags on a rest day, Dad stayed with Cowley, who loaded the bases with two outs. Ozzie Guillén stepped up, and Joe walked him, forcing in the winning run. Three straight one-run defeats, two straight walk-off defeats. It put us into last place, but still only four and a half games out.

We were down and frustrated, but the difference between winning and losing was so small. Plus, the guys who started injured, like Rickey and Winfield, were back and healthy. We all felt bad for Dad, that we let him down. None of it was his fault. But we would have run through walls for him just like Rusty Staub had tried to in '73. What nobody knew, though, was that Dad became a lame duck during that game. During the middle innings, George, who like most bullies couldn't fire people face-to-face, called Clyde King—who had once been fired as the manager and replaced by Billy—and ordered him to do the dirty work, right after the game ended.

That wasn't a great day for me in any case. I'd just been told by the doctor that I had a broken finger and would be out for a while. We were in the clubhouse, angry about the loss, and few even noticed that Clyde had gone into Dad's office. A few minutes later, PR director Joe Safety came to each locker with a four-paragraph statement confirming that, promise aside, George had given Dad—Mr. Yankee—exactly the same treatment he did Billy Martin. He decided "in the best interests of the club" to fire him and rehire...Billy Martin, who obviously had no problem swallowing his pride and suffering more indignity being George's favorite whipping boy. Trying to soften the sting for Dad, George offered the lame cliché that he "would rather fire twenty-five players than to fire Yogi, but we all know that would be impossible." Of course, the question was, why fire anyone?

When guys read the statement, the papers were thrown on the floor and the dank air was stabbed with cursing and screaming, most loudly by Donnie and Don Baylor, who was another team leader. Baylor got up and kicked over a heavy metal garbage can while yelling, "Bullshit!" over and over, then stormed off into the shower room, blood in his eyes. Donnie, unable to keep himself from making a similar scene, went into the trainer's room. There, he threw another garbage can against the wall with a crash that reverberated all around the locker room. All around guys were just affixed to their stools, not knowing what to say or do. Rickey kept muttering, "Shame... shame...shame."

My first reaction was to be with Dad. I made my way into his office while the other guys waited for me to come out, so that I could see him before anyone else did. Dad was in his uniform underwear, shoes off, calm and dignified—the classic yogi, in all situations. It was the complete opposite of Howard Schnellenberger stomping out of the locker room when Timmy's Colts fired him. I asked him if he was okay.

"I'm fine," he said quietly. "You have your future ahead of you. Mine is behind me. I've had my career. Now I want you to go have a great career."

It hit me that he was thinking about me, not himself. After all the happy moments we shared in spring training, the hugs, the smiles, he wanted me not to let personal emotions interfere with playing for Billy. "Billy's like an uncle to you; he'll be fair. Go out and play hard for him. I'll be watching you." At that moment, I knew one thing: my father was a great man, and he didn't deserve any of this. "But what about you, Dad? You gonna be all right?"

Another grin. "Why not? Tomorrow I'll be on the golf course."

He was the only one in that clubhouse who wasn't mad. I came out of there crying. So were some other guys. And if it hadn't been for Yogi telling them what he told me, calming everyone, I don't know how Billy could have managed the team. Willie Randolph, who had seen ten managers fired in ten years with the team, came to see him right after me, followed by Winfield, who gave Dad a big hug, and Donnie, who was the most upset of all. I looked up and saw him leave the office with tears in his eyes. Butch Wynegar, a high-strung guy, was also extremely upset.

We all dressed in silence, like zombies. Then, we left to catch the team bus for the ride to the airport. And that's when something amazing happened. Dad actually got on the bus and sat in the manager's seat. He didn't say a word, but he wanted to take a last ride with us, before we would go our own ways at the airport, where he'd catch a flight to Newark, we to Texas. On the ride, guys shook his hand, told him how much they appreciated him and how bad they felt about letting him down. He wouldn't hear of it. He said we'd be a winning team, to go kick some ass. We got to his gate first, and as he stood up to get off, everyone spontaneously stood and applauded him. He stepped down, took his bag from the rack, and began to walk away, a solitary figure carrying his own bag. We were still continuing our ovation for him, and hearing it, he stopped and looked back at us. As we pulled away from the curb, he stood there waving. It's hard to put into words what I felt watching him wave to us, getting smaller in the distance as the bus pulled away. All I could do was stare out the window, tears rolling down my cheek. It was like a scene from a tearjerker movie, the plot for me being that my dream of playing for my father, and his dream of managing the Yankees to a title, ended as if with a kick in the gut. And while he didn't show it, I knew that under the surface, he was hurting as much as I was.

The media had a frenzy with the firing and the story of Billy's fourth go-around. But what had been done to Dad felt to many writers like a crime had taken place. *Sports Illustrated*'s story was titled OH NO, NOT AGAIN. The brash *Daily News* sports columnist Mike Lupica penned a column headlined LYING BOSS, THY NAME IS DIRT, writing that Steinbrenner had "the soul of a used-car salesman," was "a smirking loudmouth from Cleveland" who "came to town 12 years ago and . . . contaminated a tradition," and that if "a man's word is everything, then this person who is the principal owner of the Yankees is nothing." There was also a line that went around that baseball needed Steinbrenner the way Jesus needed Judas.

Dad may well have shared those feelings, but he never would have used words like that. He had always taken George for what he was, good and bad—he had been convicted in 1974 for illegal campaign contributions to Richard Nixon and later, in 1990, would be suspended from baseball for life after paying a gambler to dig up dirt on Dave Winfield during a feud over money (he was reinstated three years later). But with it all, Dad would say, "You know what? Steinbrenner wants to win," and for that, he could cut him slack. But he had no intention of ever going back to Yankee Stadium. He made that promise to himself, and, unlike George, he intended to keep it.

LARRY: When George fired him, Dad was very quiet. He never had a bad thing to say about George. All he ever said was all he has to do is personally apologize to me and I'll forget all about it. That's it. He never insulted Steinbrenner, never called him names. You could tell he was hurt, but Dad was well beyond sulking. He was the better man, and he showed it. He wasn't naïve. He knew what he was getting into with George. It took a lot to piss him off. But George found that way, by lying to him.

He was calm. But Mom wasn't. It was déjà vu all over again for her, too. She'd never forgiven Ralph Houk for firing him in 1964, never spoke to him, and was still mad at him long after his death. She was even madder at George, because Dad was no novice manager; he'd led two teams to the World Series. You don't treat a man like that like he was yesterday's trash. She told Dad, "Yogi, don't you ever go to that ballpark or step foot in that stadium again." He had that fatalistic attitude that you can't change things, so you just move ahead. But she wouldn't let go of it, and because he worshiped her, he would begin to feel that way more and more, to the point it was set in stone. So it became personal, which was very rare for him.

He was also influenced by John McMullen, his best friend, who owned the Houston Astros and New Jersey Devils. John was the perfect example of the kind of person who loved Dad. John was seven years older than Dad, a Jersey guy, lived in Montclair his whole life. He got degrees from MIT in naval architecture and engineering, became a multimillionaire, and, with his love of sports, owned those two professional franchises. But before that, he'd been a minority owner of the Yankees. And when Dad was fired, he commiserated, saying, "Nothing was so limited as being one of George's limited partners." He went further with Dad, slamming George as a son of a bitch, saying that he had a lot of balls to fire him and that Dad should never go back to that stadium again. When people Dad admired put a bee in his bonnet, he would say, "You know, you're right."

John also gave Dad a job as a coach in Houston in '86. And wasn't it just like Dad to bring the Astros luck. That year, they would win ninety-six games and get to the National League

Championship Series before losing to the Mets in a six-game war. Dad may have looked a bit out of place in that old Astros orange and yellow sunburst uniform, but then again, it was always sunny when Dad was around. And, thanks to John, his son would soon enough be wearing that same uniform.

Billy, of course, had a very difficult task when the dust settled. He knew he'd be seen by many fans, writers, and players as having betrayed Dad, maybe even conspired to get him fired so he could have the job again. His first remarks didn't help. Trying to walk that fine line, he said, "Guys were upset about Yogi and that's O.K. Yogi was their friend. Well, I've been Yogi's friend for 35 years, and the reason he had to leave was that they put him in last place. I don't want any friends like that. I want winners." That was his way of not calling Dad a loser. But it's not the greatest thing for players to be called losers by their own manager.

One of the first things Billy did was take me aside. And, as Dad had said, there was no reason for me to hold a grudge. Billy couldn't have been kinder to me. He said, "Dale, you know how much I love your dad and how much I love your mom and your family. You're all special to me. All you have to do is go out and play the same way you did for your dad. We need you to play that way." So we got off to a good start, and that helped calm the waters with the other guys. And George, to his credit, also made sure to come to me and tell me I was a valued member of the team. "Dale," he said, "you just keep on playing like you've been playing." How much of that was guilt about Dad I don't know.

Billy continued to support me. The pressure to win, personal ambition, and the emotions of very strong-willed men can make even the sanest people lose their heads and say dumb things. But while I rode the bench, Billy would come over to me a lot and start telling me stories about Dad. A pitcher would strike out a lot of guys and he'd say, "For Chrissake, I wish your old man was here. If he ever threw those pitches to your old man, he'd hit them so far, they couldn't find them. No one could throw a fastball by your dad. Nobody."

Billy made his own changes, mostly cosmetic. Dad had no dress code, as long as we were presentable. Billy said he had to wear coats and ties on the road. We had to be in our hotel rooms three hours after a night game or by midnight after a day game. No golf or public appearances on game days. No radios without headsets. Mandatory attendance at off-day workouts—Dad had left that up to each player. There'd be a $500 fine for a first offense, $1,000 for a second, $1,000 and a suspension for a third. He also said he would have rules on drug abuse, though he never did. It didn't matter, anyway. I had resolved when I signed with the Yankees not to do any coke during the season, and I didn't. I didn't want any possible complications for Dad, and I treated being with the Yankees as a new beginning, to wipe the slate clean. Not that I was going clean and sober in general. I was just going to wait until after the season when I got home, safe in my own little refuge.

That was another rationalization, another justification. Before, my thinking was *You don't see me doing it on a game day, during a game, or before a game. I'll do it all winter long, but who cares? I'm not playing, so that's fine, that's okay.* Now, I just cut out all the in-season use. I was incredibly anal-retentive about what

I did, always on time, always where I should be. So I wouldn't allow myself to ease up. I didn't care who was doing it or not. I'm sure there were guys on the Yankees who smoked pot every day, and I'm sure there were guys who did a lot of coke, too. I just didn't pay attention to it.

We really didn't need boot camp rules, just warmer weather. After Dad's firing, we lost two more in a row in Texas, but then when the calendar turned to May, we did what we would have done anyway for Dad. We stopped making dumb mistakes, made big plays, hit in the clutch, and had great starting pitching and Rags as the closer. The down side for me was that, after my hot start, I couldn't add much. It wasn't from the effects of cocaine. It was my bat. It just died on me. After my finger healed, Billy gave me every chance to stay in the lineup. He dropped me from the seventh hole to the eighth, my old accustomed spot, and I had my good days. I had two hits and two RBIs in a 6-5 walk-off win over the Texas Rangers on May 15, the first of two straight walk-off wins, but otherwise I kept sinking.

On that roller-coaster ride down, I just seemed to be skunked. In mid-May, while we were in Kansas City, Donnie and I went over to eat in a restaurant Lou Piniella owned in Country Club Plaza. While walking back to the hotel, nature called, and since there was no bathroom nearby, we both took a leak behind a Dumpster. Hey, when you gotta go, right? When I finished, I felt a hand pulling me backward. Not knowing who it was, I instinctively tried to get free, yanking my arm in the air. Next thing I knew, both Donnie and I were being handcuffed, and I was pushed down to the street, my head pushed against the concrete. Both of us were arrested and charged with indecent conduct and me with assaulting a cop! All for taking a leak behind a Dumpster. Later, after we were released, we learned that the area was notorious for cops making arrests for public urination. Just our luck.

Naturally, the incident was all over the papers the next day. But the whole thing was a joke. We had been wrong to take a leak in public, yes, but the cops were wrong not identifying themselves and overreacting like we were criminals. The assault charge was dropped, and George told Donnie and me to pay the fine and just be done with it. It was a minor thing, almost comic relief. But then, a much more serious development arose when the other shoe dropped in the Pittsburgh drug investigation.

Word had broken that indictments were about to be handed down and that, as one report read, it could include "the biggest name in Pittsburgh sports." Whoever that was supposed to be, and it could only be Willie Stargell, it was a load of bullshit. No player was in danger, since we all had been given immunity, and Pops wasn't even called. But it was a taste of the hysteria that was to come. By the end of May, seven people were indicted on charges of dealing drugs, including Curtis Strong, who was fired by the Pirates days before, and Shelby Greer.

The trial of Curtis Strong would be in September, and the same players who testified the previous winter would be called again for the trial, with reporters allowed in this time. Anything we said about our drug usage would be magnified. If anyone had missed the sordid story over the winter, they got a face full of it now that it was all out in the open. That included my family.

LARRY: Even at that time we didn't know how heavily involved Dale was, if at all. If he was caught on the outside; was he on the inside, we didn't know. We tried to put it out of our minds. He said I'm fine, don't worry about it. And he just went right on playing, so we believed him. We just assumed he'd learned his lesson and all that shit was in the past. As long as he was okay, healthy, that was all we cared about.

But with Dad's firing and not seeing a lot of action, my mind wasn't totally focused. I pretty much wasted away all summer as I sat in the dugout game after game. By July, my average was down to .235 and the lack of regular action left me progressively stale. Billy was as disappointed as me. He would sit with me on the airplane or see me sitting on the bench, sit next to me, and say, "Goddamn it, kid, I wish I could play you, but I can't."

"I understand, Billy," I would say, thinking of Pags. "That kid's playing his ass off. He plays a great third base."

He'd repeat, "You know I love you, right?" And I'd say yeah, Billy, I know, I understand. Then he'd walk down the bench, and every time he'd pass me he'd grab my knee and say, "You all right, kid?" He loved me, yet he couldn't play me, and it was killing him.

One game I did play, it figures I was involved in one of the most bizarre plays ever. I was on first and Meacham on second when Rickey hit a ball that bounced against the left center field wall. I knew it was over the center fielder's head, so I was off and running. But Bobby thought it was going to be caught, so he went back to second to tag up. I didn't even look at him. I just ran like hell, and when I got to second I was shocked to be literally on top of him. If he'd read it right, we both would have scored standing up. But I had to stop until he saw the ball rolling around and belatedly started running. As we came around third, I was just feet behind Bobby. The relay throw came in to Carlton Fisk, who was blocking the plate. Fisk tagged Bobby out, then turned around and saw me as I tried to crash into him. We both went down in a heap and he came up holding the ball. Double play. Right out of *The Twilight Zone*. That whole season was.

When the trial in Pittsburgh got under way in September, I got my subpoena and on the ninth, I was back on the stand. It came out right away that I testified I'd purchased cocaine from Curtis Strong and got greenies from Willie Stargell. That led to some ridiculously irresponsible headlines such as DID STARGELL DISPENSE DRUGS? I fully understand why Pops denied what I said. But when you're subpoenaed, you tell the truth. I'm sure Pops understood what I had to do.

As a footnote, I got to be Rod Scurry's teammate once more. After the bad publicity of the trial, the Pirates didn't wait to get rid of him, trading him on September 14 to the Yankees, who, to their credit, had no objection to having two of the "Pittsburgh 11" on the roster. Rod did okay as a middle reliever. But his worst days were ahead of him.

In the end, Strong and six other dealers, all guys I'd bought from, were convicted, most serving a year or two in prison, though Strong got four years. While the players weren't on trial, baseball had to take a stand. By 1986, it had come to light that twenty-one players in all were involved in some way with cocaine use. Commissioner Peter Ueberroth chose to suspend the original eleven for a year, requiring us to go to drug rehab program. But when all was said and done, we never served a day of suspension or attended a single rehab session; instead, we wound up paying 10 percent of our salaries to drug programs and did community service, mainly lecturing at schools on the evils of drugs. We never had to take any blood or urine tests to see if we were clean, because of pressure by the players' union. Looking back, that was wrong.

We got off too lightly. But the fans really didn't care, anyway. Keith Hernandez was given a brief suspension by the Mets, and when he returned to the lineup the fans gave him a standing ovation. Nobody held it against us. If they had, it might have slapped some sense into me. Instead, it didn't even leave a mark. I still was convinced I wasn't so big of a coke user that I needed to stop permanently, and I didn't believe I was being a hypocrite lecturing about drugs because, in my mind, if not in my words to kids, I wasn't hooked. I was responsible. I could handle it. I just having some fun when I did it. The rationalizations continued.

But, unfortunately, so did my seeming hibernation inside the Yankee dugout as they continued their surge, getting into the race over the summer of '85, going 38-18 over July and August and entering the last month in second place, five games back. It was still the Yankees and Billy Martin, so there was drama and craziness. Some guys never did get over the trauma of Dad's firing. And others just couldn't get along with Billy.

163

Exhibit A was Ed Whitson. He was an emotional guy, and it affected his pitching. When he had some rough outings at Yankee Stadium, Billy tried to relieve the pressure by pitching him only on the road, which Eddie thought was insulting. And then when we went to Baltimore in late September, Billy took him out of a scheduled start on the road, too. Two days later, on a Saturday night, several of us went to the bar in the Cross Keys Hotel. Billy was there, too, where only the day before he'd gotten into a shouting and shoving match with some guy. I was with Leigh, who'd made the trip with me, and when Billy saw us he called, "Hey, buddy, come on over here." And as we were talking, we heard noise from the other side of the room, where Ed was at a table with someone, and they were yelling at each other.

Billy didn't want any of his players to get into an altercation in a bar—hell, he'd been in enough of those and gotten into trouble because of it. So he went over trying to be a peace-maker, calm things down. He asked me to go with him, and as soon as we got to the table, Ed turned his fire on Billy. "You son of a bitch, you're fucking trying to ruin me," he said. Billy, tensing up like an animal sensing a predator, said, "What are you talking about, Hillbilly?"—using the nickname he had for Ed, who was from Tennessee.

Ed repeated what he'd said, then without warning leaped from his seat. Again, Billy didn't want to fight. He wanted to be supportive, save Ed from trouble. But, let's face it, as nice as Billy was, especially to me, anyone could see how crazy he could get when provoked, how volatile. And he proved it right there. They exchanged a few more insults, tensions escalated, and before you knew it, the two of them were fighting. Billy had his famous fists flying, but Whitson, a big, tough kid who towered over him, was kicking Billy with his pointy-toed cowboy boots, aiming at Billy's junk and other parts.

Now I tried to be a peacemaker, although my first reaction was to side with Billy. So I grabbed Eddie by the shoulders, but it was like riding a bucking bronc. I couldn't do anything but watch as they kept brawling in slow motion across the room, knocking chairs over and sending bottles and glasses crashing, and people were ducking. It spread to the lobby, into the elevator, and up to other floors. Every time they were separated, they broke free and started up again. It finally broke up before the National Guard had to be called in. Billy and Ed went to the hospital and got stitched up, all the while being kept apart.

The next morning, both looked like they'd been through a meat grinder. Billy had a broken bone in his arm, a punctured lung, and bruises all over. Whitson had a cracked rib and a split lip, the usual souvenir of fighting with Billy. It was page one news in the papers, and Billy was worried that George would fire him if he thought he'd started a fight with one of his own players. His arm was in a sling and he looked awful—he joked that he would have won the fight but didn't know he'd be fighting a mule—but the first thing he did was come to me for help.

"Dale," he said, "you have to tell these people what you saw."

And that's what I did. I told the press Billy was trying to defuse a bad situation, and Ed clocked him. I don't know if George believed that. It probably wasn't coincidental that Ed would be with the Yankees and Billy wouldn't after the season ended. Neither did Billy suspend Ed "for the rest of his life," as he promised to do, though he did for the rest of the season. After all, you can't be using your manager as a kickboxing opponent.

I suppose at this point I should answer an obvious question. Yes, Billy drank. More than a little. He came from a time when Mickey eased all his anxieties and killed time by getting sloshed. Billy had a drinking problem like Mickey, and I don't think he ever had it under control. It was sort of like me and cocaine. I thought I could do it because I never let it affect my dedication and focus on the game. And never did I see Billy in the dugout during a game drunk, or anything less than mentally sharp.

However, I'll admit, we never saw Billy until moments before the game. Dad used to be there all the time, behind the cage during batting practice, walking in the outfield, hitting fungoes. He'd encourage guys, pat them on the butt, and say, "We're gonna get 'em today." That wasn't Billy's style. He didn't care about anything but the nine innings that counted. He mostly stayed inside his office, the door locked. He had a private bodyguard—none other than Willie Horton, the beefy former Tigers outfielder who'd played for Billy in Detroit and had 325 lifetime homers (and today is special assistant to the Tigers' president). If any of us wanted to talk to Billy before the game, we'd be stopped dead in our tracks by Willie. "Not now," he'd say, in his deep voice, his arms crossed, guarding the door. "You ain't goin' any farther than right here."

What Billy may have been doing in there, only he knew. We didn't think it was our business. And we sure as hell weren't going to try to go through Willie Horton to find out.

The funny thing is, the blowout in Baltimore didn't affect the team in the slightest. We kept rolling. We won the Sunday game 5-4, helped by back-to-back homers by Rickey and Ken, completing the season series with the Orioles winning twelve of thirteen. Then, after a loss in Detroit, we won six in a row, two on walk-offs, Gator and Phil Niekro a great one-two punch, Gator throwing fire, Phil dancing knucklers. That put us three games back of the Blue Jays with three to go, and we closed the season with three in Toronto, so we had our own destiny in our hands. In the opener, we trailed 3-2 in the top of the ninth. Butch homered to tie, then an error put us ahead and we won 4-3, getting us a game closer. We needed another two wins to tie the race, but the Jays won 5-1 on Saturday to clinch. We ended in second place, two games behind, winning ninety-seven games, six more than the Western Division–winning Kansas City Royals, who went on to win the World Series. That was the second time a team of mine had won close to 100 games and finished out of the money.

It was a hell of a ride. Gator went 22-6. Mattingly hit .324 with a league-high 145 RBIs and won the MVP. Rickey hit .314 and stole eighty bases. I still don't know how that team could have won the way it did with Steinbrenner. Every day was a new quake. And, who knows, maybe Dad could have gotten us over the finish line. If so, maybe I wouldn't have been an after-thought at the end, my rear end glued to the bench, my final average .229, one homer, eight RBIs. For the Berras, it was a season to forget. What began as a storybook fantasy ended as a slap in the face. But, within that year, the fleeting days I had wearing Yankee pinstripes with my father were the best days of my life.

CHAPTER 8

Going, Going, Gone

AS RESPECTFUL AS Billy had been with me, I knew I had no future with the Yankees. And, as if confirming why it was such an ordeal for all of us to deal with the constant storm of criticism and threats from George, even winning ninety-seven games couldn't save Billy from another unceremonious firing right after the season, this time replaced by Lou Piniella, who himself would go the route of Dad and Billy—after winning ninety and eighty-nine games, but not the division. When the team struggled in '88, he'd get the gate midway through the season; two years later, managing the Reds, he'd win the World Series.

I wouldn't play much for Lou, either. I wasn't in his plans for the team, which was his right. He kept me on the roster in '86 but with the same staleness and splinters from sitting so much, I managed to hit .231 with two homers and thirteen RBIs. Still, I felt Lou wasn't being fair with me. I could play great for a week, then do one thing wrong and not play the next week. And George would criticize you, not to your face but in the papers, like with Dad. That's very unhealthy for a team, because the manager can't have any patience with players on the bubble like me. It was Lou's first managing job, and he had to do what Dad had refused to, pull guys he wanted to play. Even Dave Winfield didn't start every game. It looked to me that they were giving away the pennant. The Yankees did a lot of that in the '80s when they had championship-level teams. It wasn't until George finally drew back in the '90s and delegated more authority to his sons that they achieved what our teams never could.

Of course, I wasn't in the same category of Winfield, so I was expendable. On July 27, I was released, making me a free agent. Lou basically told me the same thing Billy and George always had: they would have loved to keep me, but they had a winning hand, or so they thought, and it would be better for me to go to a team that could really use me. Ed Keating, after calling around to gauge interest in me, decided the best shot would be with the Astros. John McMullen was willing to sign and unite me again with Dad in 1987. My contract still had three years to run, and my salary was $657,000 in '86 and would be $757,000 in '87, so it benefited George to have another team pick up a portion of it, even though John, a very smart businessman, paid nothing the first year and less than $100,000 of it the second.

It would be hard to rival the off-season of '84–'85, but '86–'87 was close. The day after Christmas, my first child, a daughter named Whitney, was born. That was as life-changing as anything a man can ever experience, far bigger than stepping into a batter's box in the big leagues. Fatherhood had entered the picture, requiring me to be more responsible, and I was ready for it. I loved her, she was Daddy's little girl, and

I did everything a stay-at-home dad could do, feeding, bathing, changing. I'd read to her, sing to her. Dad and Mom, who already had grandkids, would look after them all the time; they loved when my brothers and I brought all our kids over. His family was his great pride, the glue of his life. And, after raising three rambunctious boys, it was like a whole new life to look after girls. I'm sure if he'd had daughters, he wouldn't have let them out of the house until they were thirty-five. And maybe he was right about that.

And yet, I'm ashamed to say, as good as I felt, I still needed to feel better. I'd been clean and sober the entire '86 season and believed I could just do some coke over the winter. And so I did. Of course, I was again conning myself, being stupid. How stupid? I might have even used it the night before or the night after one of my community service talks at area schools about drugs. It may seem like I was being a hypocrite, a dick, purposely blowing smoke in the faces of those kids. But that's not how I felt. I took it seriously, put a lot of thought into what I said. Those kids knew I'd had a problem, so they listened. In my mind, it didn't matter that I still did some, because the con was that I controlled it, that I didn't have a problem.

The message was good and sincere. It's not like I wanted kids to think I was just going through the motions of fulfilling community service. I was honest, at least up to a point. I wasn't going to tell them, "You know what, kids? I just did a gram of coke. You can do that, too!" But I wanted the overall message of controlling your own lives to get through to them, because it's good, sound advice. Drugs were part of that control—stay away, I told them, don't ruin your life, it's just starting. I remember telling them the biggest regret of my life was using drugs, even though I still hadn't learned that fully. I told them drugs were like playing Russian roulette. Don't ever take the chance; it's not worth it. And I never thought I was being dishonest, because my rationalization was that I hadn't ruined my life. Yet.

It turned out that I didn't get to see Dad much in '87. When I got to spring training at the Astros' camp in Kissimmee, Florida, I could see that Dad was much more relaxed there. John McMullen paid him his manager's salary, which was far more than any coach in the game, and I think out of respect for Dad John gave me another shot to make it. John obviously was very, very good to the Berra family.

But after the spring games, I didn't make the big club and was sent to the Astros' Tucson Triple-A team in the Pacific Coast League. That was like old times, only I wasn't on the way up; I was on the way down, and I wasn't even thirty. It was all I could do to get my head into that old minor league mind-set of clawing competition. There were a couple of older guys on the team, like Danny Driessen, a valuable member of the Big Red Machine in the '70s, who had started playing five years before me but just couldn't quit; at that age, the memories of fame and fortune are as much an addiction as anything else. At the other end of the spectrum, Duane Walker, who was my age, had played only three seasons outside the bushes.

I wasn't the oldest, but I definitely was the highest paid. And I was in a kind of no-man's-land, splitting time between shortstop, second base, third base, and even the outfield. That's what you do when your options are down to almost nothing. It was a long way from Houston, where Dad had the year before helped the Astros run away with their first division title. I would have loved to have been in Houston with Dad, playing behind Nolan Ryan and Mike Scott, the '86 Cy Young winner who almost got them to the World Series only to see the team lose in that unbelievable game 6 to the Mets. Dad was sure Scott would have won a game 7. He was the best pitcher in the league for a couple years, many say partly because he learned how to scuff the ball.

A few pitchers did it, guys who knew how to do it and not get caught. They'd glue a tiny piece of sandpaper on the tip of a finger on their glove hand, just a speck, and if an ump came out to search them they'd flick it off. No one would even see it. Don Sutton went to the Hall of Fame scuffing the ball. Rick Rhoden did it. I also played with Joe Niekro, who was famously caught when he used a nail file and tried to throw it away. And Scott could make a ball do whatever he wanted and still throw it ninety miles per hour. The bottom would drop out, three or four inches. You can't hit that.

It was easier to hit in the minors. I had a decent enough season in Tucson. I had gotten my stroke back and was playing good defense. I was in 116 games, mostly at third and short. I hit .270, with nine homers and fifty-nine RBIs, and even stole eleven bases. I also *pitched*, or rather, mopped up, getting the final out of one lopsided game. (We won't talk about the twenty-five errors I made at third.) I felt sort of young again—it helped that one of the guys on that team was Davey Lopes, the former Dodgers speedster who was forty-two and doing anything he could to hang on.

In fact, both of us were called up because the Astros were in the thick of the race and, just like Chuck Tanner had done years before, the manager, Hal Lanier, believed I could help win him a pennant by stepping in for a regular who was injured, in this case shortstop Craig Reynolds. My manager at Tucson, Bob Didier, who they called "Diddy Ball," a former big-league catcher, called Hal to specifically recommend that I be called up. He said I was tearing it up, playing a very good shortstop, and I could do the job. And so Hal, like Chuck, put me right in when I got to Houston.

I was raring to go, too, but my body didn't cooperate. I was all right, no more. I started sixteen games at short, made just two errors, but couldn't compensate for big-league pitching, hitting only .178 with two RBIs. Dad knew I was frustrated. He was his usual optimistic self, encouraging me, telling me to hang in. We'd go to dinner and go over the next day's pitcher, but mostly he'd keep my mind off the game talking about Whitney and fatherhood. I never loved that man more than I did then, seeing how much he was hurting for me. And I never felt as ashamed as I did then, keeping from him the major cause of my falling from the guy who'd played such a crucial role in the pennant drive for the "We Are Family" Pirates and been so dependable for 161 games in 1983.

My skills had eroded, to the point where I couldn't be successful on the big-league level, and not coincidentally, my cocaine use was escalating. I was learning one thing through painful experience: cocaine was killing me in more ways than physical. It was killing my bond with my family, my parents, my wife, my daughter. And yet I still couldn't muster up the courage to end it and finally act like a grown-up—like Yogi Berra's son. Instead, I began making exceptions to my in-season rule. I'd get some coke to do on off days, or on the day after a night game. Just a little, here and there. Just to feel a little better. Using the whole inventory of excuses, I was okay. After all, I just wanted to have fun, not to make myself feel better.

By now, there was a real stigma to having been unmasked as a cocaine user. Despite the kid-glove treatment given the Pittsburgh 11, we all wore a scarlet letter. And more and more, news would break about some tragic consequence of using the drug. Long before Ken Caminiti's shocking demise—after battling booze and coke in his fine career, mainly with the Astros, and doing time in jail for possession, he died in 2004 after injecting a speedball of coke and heroin, the same concoction that killed John Belushi—there was Rod Scurry. I didn't have much contact with him in New York, but he seemed okay, no talk about snakes crawling all over him. He played on the Giants' Triple-A team in '87, then signed with the Seattle Mariners. Released again in December 1988, he was busted for coke possession in a Las Vegas crack house. Four years later, out of the game, he was arrested after acting strangely outside his home, screaming about his old bugaboo—the snakes, which he said were eating him. When cops were cuffing him, he collapsed. After a week on life support, he died at thirty-six.

I felt terrible when I heard that. I liked Rod. He was a friend of mine, a good teammate. He had a real problem, one that cost him his life. But, to be honest, I didn't feel it was a lesson for me. I didn't have the same problem. My problem cost me a career, not my life. So it would have taken a lot more than what happened to Rod to scare me. Not even seeing my career flushed down the john could do that. Because even when that was happening, I still conned myself that I was okay, just a good-time guy. Not in a million years would I have done what

Scurry had. I would never have smoked crack or, God knows, stick a damn needle in my arm. I never had a monkey on my back, didn't need Valium to come down, didn't vacuum the rug at three a.m. because I couldn't sleep. You would never know I was hooked on anything but baseball. That was my secret victory. But there was nothing victorious about it.

Neither was there anything victorious about the Astros when all was said and done. They went from being contenders in August to falling out of the race in September. I think Hal appreciated the fact that I didn't quit. I always was juiced to get out there and play hard. It was just that my body didn't cooperate. Even so, when the Astros released me after the season, I believed it could be a good break. Maybe I needed to be away from the umbrella of my father, perhaps become a designated hitter in the American League. That could be a fresh start. And I wasn't the only one in the game who thought that way. Over the winter, the Baltimore Orioles came to Ed Keating with an offer to become a player-coach with their Triple-A team in Rochester, New York. That was flattering that a team could still see something in me, and that it I could salvage my career, give me a foot in the door of coaching and maybe, down the road, managing.

If I could do that, I would get further than the other guys who were caught up in the drug scandal. Most of them were winding down their careers by then, but they were older than me. I was still only thirty and should have had another five, six years, maybe good years. But now it was beyond doubt that coke had eaten into my reflexes. Just a tiny, split-second drop-off in your reaction time in swinging at a pitch or picking up the angle of a ball hit off the bat—which looks like a blur in any case—is fatal to a baseball player.

But coke had a hold on me. If I knew it on a subconscious level, I still refused to admit it. I hid behind the external circumstances, judging my descent as the result of playing so little. But it quickly became apparent that I couldn't save my career. That Rochester team was really good, managed by Johnny Oates, a pretty good catcher who'd begun his managing career in the Yankees chain and would win the Western Division of the International League that season, preceding what would be a successful eleven-year run managing in the majors. Johnny gave me every chance. I played sixty-nine games, and he put me in at every infield position and to mop up four games on the mound. But my bat was certifiably dead, capable of hitting only .181 with three homers and thirteen RBIs, in sixty-nine games.

That, sadly, would be my swan song. Before I reached my thirty-second birthday, I retired. In retrospect, it hadn't been a bad run. I'd come up when I was almost as young as Dad was when he did, and I played four years less than he had. I had no bitterness, but I did have regrets, knowing I should have been a lot better. Unfortunately, the regrets didn't yet include the damaging effects cocaine had on me, which I knew deep down but couldn't admit to myself. When I came home for the winter, I again cranked up my cocaine use. And it landed me in a lot more trouble and embarrassment.

◇ ◇ ◇ ◇

When you do drugs, you naturally fall in with the wrong people. It's not by choice, only convenience. I had more time on my hands now. I wouldn't have to gear up for another season right after the New Year. I had no real plans. I could have gone deeper into coaching, but I needed time to think about it. The thought of being away from home, and not being able to play, to put on a uniform that never got dirty or sweaty, seemed as exciting as watching paint dry. When Dad was a coach, he said the best part of the job was working with players between games, and the worst part was basically doing nothing on game days. He would even grab a bat and hit fungoes during infield practice, just to do something active. I couldn't see myself doing that. He was in his forties when he took the Mets coaching job. I was in my early thirties. How many years might I have to put in before maybe getting a chance to manage? I had better things to do with my life, by just living it.

Then, too, while I still loved the game, I wanted to decompress from the grind of two decades concentrating all of my energy on baseball. And as I looked down the horizon, cocaine should not have been part of that process. But it was.

I worked at a few things, but then I decided to just kick back. I had enough money from baseball, so my life was a cycle of partying and watching sports at bars with a gram of coke. In the summertime we'd be at the Jersey shore, constantly partying. And it didn't take long before I found myself in trouble for the second time, for buying some coke from a guy who was being watched by the police. I suppose that's an occupational hazard when you use illegal drugs. I was terribly naïve to think that there weren't a thousand guys just like Curtis Strong, guys who could get me into trouble. This one's name was John Bailey. Someone told me about him and gave me his number. All I knew about him was he sold grams to people from his apartment in Morristown, and I became another customer. The stuff was good, and so I called him—big mistake—and asked, "Can I call you when I need to?" Later, I heard myself ask that on a police wiretap of Bailey's phone.

Not long after, two plainclothes cops from Glen Ridge came to my home at eight in the morning—shades of the FBI coming to Dad's door four years before. They had a warrant for my arrest. I said, "For what?" They said cocaine possession. I let them in, and they searched me and the house. Leigh and Whitney were home. Fortunately, Whitney was asleep, but Leigh was terrified. She stood there speechless as the search went on. As it turned out, I had nothing, just an empty cellophane bag in my pants with remnants of cocaine. Then they said, "We have to take you," so I got into the cruiser outside and they took me to the Morristown Police Department stationhouse to process me, and that's when I found out about being caught up in a phone call with John Bailey. They had gotten me on tape two or three times and had pictures of me in the parking lot of his place. Again, I was just a guy who walked into this thing along with twenty-four other people Bailey sold coke to. I was probably the one he sold the least to, no more than a gram at a time. I never sold cocaine, never sold a drug in my life, so I knew my role was limited, although it didn't seem that way as I was fingerprinted, my mug shot was taken, and I was ushered into a holding cell.

The other twenty-four people in the ring were there, too, all of them put into the same cell. It was like the state room scene in the Marx Brothers' *Night at the Opera*. One more person and the door would break open. In a few hours, we were herded out to see a judge, who told us what the charges were: conspiracy to violate state narcotic laws, which was a broad, catchall category that could have meant anything, really. The dealers would face stiffer charges. And that was it. I was released on $5,000 bail. I was home by three in the afternoon.

Just as with the Pittsburgh grand jury, things stagnated after that, to the point where I had no idea what was happening. There wouldn't be a court proceeding for another year. The parallel with Pittsburgh was striking. Most of those people who were busted were just pawns, witnesses, not the big fish. Still, it was more serious this time because there was no immunity and there was a possibility any of us could be charged eventually with intent to sell. And I immediately hired a lawyer who began talking with the authorities about working out a deal. The worst of it was subjecting my family to this kind of nonsense again and seeing them go through the same stages of worry and bewilderment.

LARRY: I said, damn, *again*? That's where we all found out that he was deeper into it than we thought. But then it seemed like it was a big mistake. We just held our breath and hoped to ride it through.

Like Pittsburgh, the headlines of my arrest were like kicks in the gut—DALE BERRA ARRESTED FOR DRUG CONSPIRACY was a common one, with the lead paragraphs of every article giving the mandatory fact that the guy arrested was the son of Yogi Berra. That pained him, and me, as it was exactly what he had meant when he said do anything you want but don't drag the family name into something ugly. Still, he, Mom, and my brothers were completely supportive and cared only that I was all right and that I get help. And I leaned on them to get me through, lucky as a man could be that his family was willing to overlook his stupidity and recklessness. I was distraught over what I'd done to them, and my wife and daughter. That guilt will follow me to my grave. But had they not been there for me, I don't know if I'd be here writing these words today.

Although I was an easy target, Phil Pepe, the longtime sports columnist of the *Daily News*, wrote poignantly that I wasn't a bad guy, only one who, because of "whatever demons were at work inside him…apparently turned to drugs." That hurt, but it was fair, and it echoed Chuck Tanner, who said of me, "I feel sorry for him.…He was a nice young man. I don't know how he got sidetracked in his life."

I didn't blame Chuck for that; I didn't fully understand myself why I did it. Sometimes, there are only questions, not easy answers. And there are never easy solutions.

In August 1989, a Morris County grand jury delivered the indictments. The charge against me was simple drug possession and conspiracy to purchase cocaine. I was not in any drug ring. My crime was really simple stupidity. But having made such a high-visibility bust, they had to indict me for something. My lawyer had already plea-bargained, and when I stood before New Jersey Superior Court judge Peter Conforti, it was a done deal. Judge Conforti set me free, to go right into what was called a pretrial intervention program. I was fined $1,000, placed on probation, and agreed to drug testing. I'd speak at schools again about the dangers of drugs. Then, after a year, the entire case would be expunged from the record. And so that's what I did. The very next day, I was at rehab. For a year, I was clean and sober. John Bailey was indicted on serious charges. I never found out exactly what happened to Bailey after that. What I do know is that I never had anything to do with him again.

LARRY: We were relieved he was in rehab. He was getting himself together, and he spent a lot of time with Whitney being a good father. At that point, I thought he had grown up, finally become the man he needed to be. If he thought about being a coach, that wasn't going to be possible because of this crap. But he had enough money from baseball to just get himself prepared to face the rest of his life. He was enjoying living clean. That's what we thought. But we all felt like he'd had more of a problem than we thought, and that it might not be so easy.

CHAPTER 9

Requiem for a Heavyweight

JOHN MCMULLEN TOLD Dad he could keep his coaching job in Houston for as long as he wanted. He decided in 1989 that he'd give it one more year, then he'd be finally ready to retire from the game. He sure as hell didn't want to spend his golden years, when he should be enjoying himself, worrying about his stupid son. And I sure as hell didn't want to spend my transition years to a life without baseball making his life and my whole family miserable. I thought I was on the right track. I was the same guy. I was still the guy who'd be there watching at seven thirty every night the New York Rangers were on TV. The guy who watched the Giants football games with Dad. Eating dinner with Mom and Dad, or with Leigh and Whitney. Sitting with Mom and talking about my life.

How lucky was I to have them all? Dad had taken so much pain with me, he didn't deserve any of it. Yet there he was, never scolding me, only defending me. When I was arrested, I'd hear him telling friends, "Damn, that shit must be hard to get off. I had my vodka, but this must be a lot harder to quit.

But he'll be okay. He's a good kid. He's got a good heart. He never hurt nobody."

I worried not about myself but for Whitney. Fortunately, she was only three, so she would have no memory of what was going on with my life. Which was basically that it was falling apart. By the end of '89, my marriage simply could not withstand the convulsions of my personal life. The embarrassment, the humiliation, and the strains of dealing with the legal liabilities came just as Whitney was becoming more aware of the outside world. The last thing I wanted was for her to be tarred by it. And so Leigh and I divorced, and I moved out.

I'll take the blame for that. I wasn't a good husband. I thought I was, but it was an extension of my feeling that I could live a normal life when I wasn't. All parts of one's life are interrelated; fooling yourself about drugs will affect how you approach your life in general. I was living a lie, and that will destroy a marriage because the trust between two people is weakened. I'll say this, though: I didn't intentionally disrespect Leigh. Our love was real. Maybe we married too young, before we were both mature enough to handle that kind of challenge, that of a professional athlete who would be away from home so much.

I can confirm that the loneliness of living out of a suitcase is intolerable, and that the boredom combined with the temptations available to a ballplayer on the road is a dangerous mix. I saw so many guys treat their marriages like a sham, a show, and ignore relationships with their kids. Most players are selfish by nature. The arrogance of excelling in rabid competition can create a great athlete but a horrible person. It was nothing for guys to take off their wedding rings once the plane took off on a road trip, not that a ring would stop the "Baseball Annies" out there from coming on to baseball players at a hotel or a bar. They were on the prowl, and so were the players. I saw things during those nights that turned me off. I wasn't a participant in those kinds of games. I never took off my ring except during games. I wasn't a carouser or a cheater. I was there to play ball, not screw around. When I did coke, it wasn't an act of hostility against anyone. It was a way to kill time, feel good, party. I just loved the way it made me feel. Too damn good.

By the same token, I always tried to be there for Whitney. I never thought coke ever came between us. But obviously, when I look back, I didn't do enough. My rationalizations had spread to fatherhood. Whitney was too young to know what I was doing with cocaine. But coke had come between Leigh and me, and that fueled the breakup of our family. It was part of the chain. And I worried that it would break the chain I have with my own flesh and blood.

WHITNEY BERRA: There has never been a time when I thought that way. I never saw my dad play baseball, didn't know anything about him other than he was my father, and we had what seemed like a normal family. The divorce wasn't messy; they stayed friends. He knew I was very close to my mom, never tried to compete with that. We were still a family. We did things together. I went to Grammy and Grandpa's house all the time. I didn't know anything about Yogi other than he was a lovable, faith-loving man, a character, the guy with the horse and buggy outside at the curb waiting for us. My father wanted me to get to know Yogi, to get me to absorb from Yogi what he did. And he was still trying to learn from Yogi, even then.

I was shy as a kid, and so there were certain energies or people that I just like to always be around, and Yogi was just someone that I liked to be around, him and my grandmother. As I look back I see that both of them were really special, almost like enlightened beings of just love. And I feel so honored to be a part of that lineage and family, I'm actually blown away by it. There was just a lot of love in both of them. No judgments, just good people.

After the plea deal, like I said, I stayed clean for a year. It wasn't hard. It never was hard to stay off coke, because I wasn't a heavy user of it. You can't avoid becoming hooked in some way when you use drugs; the first time pulls you in. But I had consciously maintained a low level of use, so there was no great withdrawal involved. I always believed it was more of a psychological addiction than a physical one. That was a delusion, of course, but it wasn't entirely untrue. When something becomes part of your ritual, rather than a deviation, a compulsion, you handle it better. That was why I could swear off the stuff during seasons, never touch a drop until I got back home. But now I was always home.

The program included rehab, as an outpatient at my own leisure. I went to all the meetings, spoke to the psychiatrists, did community service. The conviction was wiped away. If you look for it on the books, you won't find it. I can say, and be technically accurate, that I had never been arrested. I had to go see a probation guy in East Orange once every couple of weeks. He would drug test me. I was clean. And then...well, you know what happened.

I might have kicked coke forever if I could have kicked my stupidity. But I didn't. When I completed the program, I went right back to my old ways, my old stupidity. I thought it would be okay to have a little fun again while I watched my life go by. I started having a drink or two. No harm, no foul. I was still in control. I would do maybe a gram or two. If it was six in the morning and I needed to go to bed, I'd stop, flat out. No Valium or Quaalude. No scrounging around the carpet looking for little bits of coke. I might be up for a couple of hours staring at the ceiling, but I'm not going to take a damn Valium. I told my brain, my body, to do what I wanted.

But let's face it, I wasn't in control. I'm not that good an actor. People could see something was wrong with me. There's a lot of secret-keeping when people you know see you doing drugs. It's part of the code of honor among coke users. You don't rat out one of your own. But Montclair is a small town, everyone knows everyone else, and word gets around. In my case, I had friends who cared for me, who knew I was walking on a tight-rope. If I violated probation, if I walked into trouble again, I wouldn't get off so easily the next time. I could do jail time. It would crush my family. If I wasn't smart enough to see that, my friends were. And so when word got to my brothers, that ripped it. Larry and Timmy got together with Dad and Mom and they planned a strategy. It was time for an intervention.

It happened in early 1992. I didn't know it when I woke

up that day, but it would be the last day I'd ever stick cocaine up my nose. The end of that treadmill came when the phone rang. I picked up. It was Dad. There was no hello, just a simple sentence.

"Get up and get over here. I want to talk to you."

By the sound of his voice, I knew it was serious. He was pissed off. And when he was pissed off, there was no "Okay, Dad, I'll be there in like an hour." You had to get over there, right now. I had no idea what it was about, and I was nervous because I hadn't heard that in his voice for a long time. When I got there, I walked into a tribunal. In the living room, there were Mom and Dad, Larry and Timmy. None looked happy. This wasn't going to be a normal get-together. Even so, everyone was calm. There was no yelling. My brothers spoke first, the gist of it being, we love you and we want you to be our brother. I could see, feel, how much they were hurting for me, but I was stubborn. I didn't want to admit I was in trouble. I was about to say, for the millionth time, that I was fine and go. And then it was Dad's turn. As ever, he was direct, blunt. No wasted words.

"I want to be your dad, but if you keep on doing this, you're not a Berra anymore. That's it."

That hit me like a fastball in the noggin. I could tell he wasn't bullshitting around. He meant it. He'd thought about it and was down to his wit's end with me. And he wanted no more of it. That was when I knew my game was up. The con was over. My resistance was already peeling away. He could see that, and he expanded on what he'd said.

"There's a lot of benefits to being a Berra, family benefits, benefits to having brothers. But you won't have any of that if

187

you do drugs again. You'll no longer be a Berra. You'll have no brothers and no mom and dad. We won't be in your life."

I never imagined my old man could speak those words. Our family was cemented together. We were rock solid. But I had cracked that wall, and I had to be the one to mend it. I don't know if Dad ever thought he could say what he did. He never had before, and every syllable killed him. Mom was crying. Larry and Timmy sat silent, waiting for me to say something.

LARRY: Dad laid down the law, and Dale was scared to death. He said, "We've been with you this long, we've stuck with you. And if anything happens again, I have two sons." He never raised his voice. He just said flat out, "I'll have two sons and you're not a part of this family anymore."

My mind was spinning. I knew I was about to change my life, that I had no other option. All I could say was, "Okay, got it," which was Yogi-like in its brevity, deep in meaning. And as funny as it sounds, my first thought was that I'd been handed a gift, a gift from God. I'd been given my life back, to restart it, push the reboot button. There wasn't a doubt in my mind that I would never do drugs or take a drink again. Never put myself in a compromising position. Never have to look over my shoulder again.

LARRY: There's an actual concept people learn when they go to AA meetings. It's called getting shot by a golden arrow. It hits you and you walk away from addiction and never go back. He walked out of the house and he never took a drug or a drink again. He says years later, "I've never even thought about it." If he's in a situation where people are drinking, he'll sit there with a club soda. He's like a health nut now. He hasn't aged a day since then. That's pretty incredible. But that was the power of family. That's his golden arrow.

TIM: Looking back, he destroyed his career but saved his life. That's the important thing. And it only happened because of what really mattered most to him, his love for his family. It wasn't rehab or public shame. He could deal with that, get around them. It was the thought of being disowned, if you want to put it that way, by the family that pulled him out of hell, brought him back to us.

My life changed on a dime. I'm not claiming any supernatural powers of self-healing, no magic formula. But I didn't need any sort of transition period. I didn't go to drug rehab because I didn't need to. I was healed by the time I walked out of the house. I never looked back. I didn't go to the bar. I went to see Whitney. I wanted her to see a father she would never need to worry about. And I wanted to see a daughter through eyes that would never be clouded again.

Neither did I go back to baseball. For a while I worked with a partner in an electrical company, but I was comfortable financially, so I really just enjoyed my life, watched my daughter grow, felt good about myself. It wasn't that I regarded the game as the root of all my evil. I love baseball, always will. But I had to make a new life for myself, and I couldn't do that in a world where everywhere I would look, there'd be a memory of something I didn't want to remember. Besides, I'd given it my best shot. I accomplished things I could be proud of. That was my dream, and I lived it. For Dad, there was a time to give it up, and for me there was, too. In my new life, I would rather coach Whitney's softball teams than any big-league team. That was a real measure of how much I'd changed.

Dad changed, too. Though in many ways, he never did. In his declining years, he would take me along to the Montclair Golf Club. He could never sit at home doing nothing, or he'd start to go a little crazy. He'd sit in the starter's booth at the club and shoot the breeze with the guy who greeted the members and their guests. Inevitably, someone would say, "Hey, did I just see Yogi Berra?" or "I can't believe I just saw Yogi Berra!" and come over and start talking to him. Other guys would say things like, "Yogi, do you remember me? When you were a kid I was in St. Louis and I remember playing ball with you." Dad would act like the guy was his best friend. Then, when the person would walk away, I'd ask him, "So who was that?" And he'd get that sly grin on his face.

"Damned if I know," he would say.

That was Dad. By the late '90s, though, I saw him become a different man during his self-imposed exile from the Yankees. I saw a man whose pride was hurting, and he let it affect his judgment. Just imagine the eddy of emotions he was going through. He had turned his back on the team he'd given so much to for four decades. He'd made his second home, Yankee Stadium, an enemy fortress, occupied by an interloper from Cleveland who represented values and behavior alien from the Yankees tradition and provoked stress and strife. He was, in effect, a man without a country, in baseball terms, stranded. He wouldn't even watch Yankees games. Invitations would be sent each year for him to come to Old-Timers' Day. Timmy and I would ask him if he would consider going. Forget about George, we'd tell him. Do it for your fans. They miss you like hell. We even had some of his old friends in the game ask him.

"No fuckin' way! I ain't goin' back!" he'd bellow. And I mean bellow. He'd be yelling at us, just for asking. That's how stubborn his pride was.

The problem was, George was the same way. He told us that Dad would have to come crawling back—something that never would have happened in a million years. Dad never crawled before anyone. It didn't matter to George that he was taking a lot of heat from the fans and the writers for Dad's exile; nobody blamed Dad, and it was easy to hate on George. He knew you can't possibly win a war with Yogi Berra in New York. But neither would he apologize openly for the way he had fired Dad, so it was the classic stalemate. Dad stood on principle, the fact that George lied to him, violating a man's most sacred bond, his word. And George stood on his ego, not ceding an inch.

The family, of course, followed Dad's lead. No one, not his sons or grandchildren, had set foot in Yankee Stadium in all that time. Dad went quite a bit to Giants Stadium to watch football games as a guest of NFL commissioner Paul Tagliabue. He also went to Shea Stadium for a Mets-Astros game, to say hello to Craig Biggio and Art Howe while he was still managing the team, guys he loved from his coaching days. However, not even Whitey Ford could change Dad's mind about coming back to Yankee Stadium. "I don't care what you think of Steinbrenner," Whitey told him, "the people miss you." But Dad wouldn't budge. When the Yankees held a day for Don Mattingly, the man Dad had fought so hard for, Donnie called him and personally asked him to attend.

"I didn't show up for Scooter's day, either," Dad told him. "Scooter understood, and you'll have to understand, too."

The closest he came to communicating with the team were regular phone calls he had with Don Zimmer, the Smurf-like ex-Brooklyn Dodger who was Joe Torre's bench coach and good luck charm, much as Dad was for Billy Martin. But Zim knew he couldn't budge Dad, so he never tried.

In '98, the Yankees retired his number 8—which he of course shared with Bill Dickey—and put up a plaque for each in Monument Park behind the center field fence in Yankee Stadium. Dad still wouldn't give in. The elderly Dickey was there, but Dad wasn't. As Mike Lupica wrote that day, "He doesn't go to Yankee Stadium anymore, which is the same as if Joe DiMaggio had exiled himself from the place. DiMaggio is known as the greatest living Yankee. If that is true, Yogi Berra is the one who is most loved...They can have all the plaques they want for him. Until he comes back...it is as if there is a whole wing of Monument Park vacant."

That year, the Yankees won their first of three straight championships, one of four in five years, restoring the kind of dynasty Dad knew so well. The torch had been passed, but many believed the past was being forgotten. After the season, Joe D died. A few days before, George had been with him. Joe had a request. As George recalled, "I got very close to Joe DiMaggio at the end. He would point that finger at me and say, 'You've got to get him back,'" the "him" being Yogi Berra. George became quite sentimental. Celebrating new championships was great, but, he said, "There was a missing piece," meaning Dad coming back to where he belonged.

Dad wasn't nearly as sentimental about it. He thought he didn't need the adulation. He got it wherever he went. During a Giants game, Lupica noted in his column, "When the people in the stands in front of Box 219B saw him, it was as if a whole section stopped watching the football game for a minute and turned and applauded." That was good enough for him. But as each year passed, he felt the weight of history on his shoulders. His circle of contemporaries shrunk. Billy in 1989 in a car accident, Mickey died in 1995, and then Joe in 1999. Dad had to go to more funerals than he could count. Each funeral, especially Mickey's—where he was a pallbearer with Whitey, Moose Skowron, Hank Bauer, Johnny Blanchard, and Bobby Murcer—carved a hole in his soul and made him confront getting old. We, his family, could not allow him to live the rest of his life embittered and isolated from all those Yankee fans. We knew he needed to be the Yogi that the world adored, the man who befriended everyone he met, who loved life, who loved the Yankees. The man about whom his old roomie Bobby Brown once said, "Every time I see him, I feel a little better about the human race."

His sanctuary during this time was the culmination of a dream that he and the family worked to bring to fruition—a Yogi Berra museum. In the late '90s, we raised $2 million from Investors Bank, John McMullen, and other donors. Construction began, and in December 1998 we opened the Yogi Berra Museum and Learning Center, on the campus of Montclair State, right next to where the school team and then a minor league team would play baseball in Yogi Berra Stadium, a fantastic place to watch a game. Dad donated practically every scrap of memorabilia he had to the museum, and every photo of himself and the family. Architects designed a scoreboard built as a precise scaled-down model of the big board in right center field in the old Yankee Stadium, displaying the innings and line score of Larsen's perfect game, even with the great old period ads emblazoned on it.

A bronze statue of Dad, clad in his "tools of ignorance," was created by sculptor Brian Hanlon and placed on the street just outside the museum, near an archway entrance with a giant facsimile of a baseball with Dad's signature. On the front of the museum are the words "The House That Yogi's Friends Built." At the opening ceremonies, Ted Williams and Larry Doby made great speeches. Ted remembered the first time he ever saw the funny-looking catcher and did a double take. "Who the hell is this guy?" he said he asked the ump. Dad, of course, didn't disappoint when he made his own remarks. "Usually when you get something like this, you're dead or you're gone," he said. Who could argue with that? He was amazed by all the images of him all around, which we dug up from every source we could. Even he hadn't seen a lot of them.

The timing of the museum was helpful in one very special way: providing the means to end the cold war with George.

That could only happen if George apologized for firing Dad as he did. If George made the first move to end the feud, we could do it. And things began to happen in '98. The time was right. George was in his mid-sixties, Dad a decade older, and it became a pressing matter to a lot of people that their feud be resolved while they were still around. One of those people was Suzyn Waldman, the Yankees' radio broadcaster. With her warmth and perky New England accent, Suzyn could get anyone to let their defenses down, and she made it her mission to bring the two stubborn warhorses together.

"Dale," she told me one day, "I think I can broker this thing. I have George's ear. Do you think you can get your dad to come back to Yankee Stadium?"

That would have been a rough one to pull off. A better way, I said, would be if George came to the museum. Dad's turf, where he'd be comfortable. Suzyn called and told me she got George to agree to it. Before I went to Dad, I ran it by Mom. Despite the hard feelings, she thought it was high time to end the grudge match and said to go ahead and ask him. But she added, "I'll do whatever your dad wants." In this situation, even her opinion wouldn't sway him. It was all up to Dad.

I sat down next to him in the living room.

"Dad, what about George coming out here and apologizing?"

"For what?" he asked.

"For firing you, so you can go back to Yankee Stadium."

"Goddamn it, no! I told you, no way! I ain't goin' back!"

I knew that if his mind could be changed, it wouldn't be for himself, his ego. But I knew what would do it.

"Dad, do you realize you have grandchildren who've never seen you in a Yankee uniform? They've never associated you with Yankee pinstripes and Yankee honor and Yankee pride. All they know is from reading or hearing about it. If you go back to Yankee Stadium again, your grandkids can see you on the field, see them honor you on the scoreboard and see your plaque."

That thought, of those kids seeing him enshrined with icons like Ruth, DiMaggio, Gehrig, and Mantle in Monument Park, had to move him. To close the deal, I added one more thing.

"And Mom says you should."

He thought a while, then waved his hand. "Okay, okay, let's get it over with."

As soon as he uttered those words, the war was over. He seemed to become calm, more so than he had been for years. Deep down, he was overjoyed that he wouldn't have to hold that bitterness inside him. It was like we had done an intervention with *him*. From there, things happened fast. In early January, George flew up from Tampa, and Suzyn escorted George into the museum for what would be the most famous day the place will ever see and the biggest making-up since Jerry Lewis buried the hatchet with Dean Martin. He was a little late, but when he got to the museum, he strode in, saw Dad waiting, and extended his hand.

"Hello, Yogi," he chirped.

Dad's first words to him after fourteen years were ones we were familiar with, having heard them at one time or another since we were tykes.

"You're late."

Dad and Mom took George into an office. Mom would later say that George reached out for both of Dad's hands and told him, "'I know I made a mistake by not letting you go personally. It's the worst mistake I ever made in baseball.'"

"I made a lot of mistakes in baseball, too," he replied.

And that was basically the end of the feud. Dad gave George a tour of his museum, the two of them answered questions from reporters, and Dad was asked if he would come back to Yankee Stadium when the season began, such as on opening day or Old-Timers' Day.

"I told him what he needed to do," he said. "He apologized. We'll see."

George added: "If I could get Yogi to come back, I'd bring him over with a rickshaw across the George Washington Bridge."

I got to put in my two cents, too. When a reporter asked me about why Dad had changed his mind, I said, "My dad never felt like he wasn't a part of the Yankee family, and would never have wanted to go back to the Stadium just for a standing ovation. I told him, 'You've got to do what you've got to do.' But fourteen years is long enough."

As always, Mom had the last and best word. She had mainly watched the reconciliation unfold before her eyes and said nothing, just enjoyed it. She knew exactly what Dad was thinking, that the feud hadn't just ended but on his terms, having

197

Mohammad come to the mountain. Almost in a whisper, she said to me, "'He's very proud of this."

Indeed, he was. The dizzying day was like a fable. When George left, the *New York Times* wrote, he was "clutching a copy of Berra's latest book of original 'Yogisms' and a Berra Museum shirt. [He] said, "I'll talk to you soon." The door closed. Dad, who coined the expression "It [ain't] over till it's over," turned back. "Fourteen years," he said, smiling. "It's over." That night, when we all had dinner, he came in walking on air. I don't know if I ever saw him happier. He'd made his point, won his war. And he was a Yankee again. Conviction was one thing, but you never lose your birthright. Just ask me about that.

It was arranged that Yogi Berra would make his long-awaited return for the home opener on April 9 against the Detroit Tigers, to throw out the first pitch. That was the role that Joe D traditionally held, and Dad was truly honored to be the Yankee idol who carried on the tradition without interruption. Dad didn't need a rickshaw to get to the Bronx. On that glorious day, Dave Kaplan, a former sportswriter who had co-written some of those books with Dad and is the founding director of the museum, took him and Mom in, and they had a ball. They both looked stunning, Dad in a tailored charcoal gray Italian (what else?) suit, and she in a white linen blouse and jacket. When he arrived, he was taken into the players gate. In the maze of musty, subterranean corridors that had been reconstructed since he last walked down them, he had to be led to the Yankee clubhouse. "I got lost," he said when he got there.

"It's a lot different than it used to be." The players stopped what they were doing to shake his hand. Smiling broadly, he made effortless conversation. As the team raised its championship flag on the center field flagpole, and then went through pre-game festivities and introductions, he waited in the dugout, sandwiched by Whitey and Zim.

Then, the voice of Bob Sheppard, the wonderfully stentorian public address announcer then eighty-nine and known as "the voice of God"—who from 1951 on had prefaced every one of Dad's regular season and World Series at-bats at home with his familiar call "Now batting for the Yankees, catcher, number 8, Yogi Berra, number 8"—stood at home plate, his voice echoing through the packed stadium. Bob spoke of Dad as "a great leader and a man of conviction." Striding to the mound, the noise deafening, Dad said later, "I was a little nervous." But, peering at catcher Jorge Posada, he threw a high strike, buried in a tidal wave of adulation. "It wasn't bad," he admitted. "I thought I'd do worse." But did Yogi Berra ever do worse?

He walked off, waving, to sit in George's VIP box and watch the Yankees win 12-3, enjoying himself immensely. He knew full well what the day had meant. As he told everyone, he was home again.

He said he'd be back for others, and he was. The same month, he was there when the Yankees unveiled the monument to Joe DiMaggio. And he was thrilled when the team revealed plans for Yogi Berra Day, on July 18. This was actually the second such Yogi Berra Day at the Stadium; the first was in 1959. Forty years later, the entire Berra family, including the nine grandchildren, boarded a ferry that had just been commissioned to take passengers across the Hudson River from and to Weehawken, New Jersey. The name of the ferry was the *Yogi Berra*. (That *Yogi* would make headlines, too. Remember the plane piloted by "Sully" Sullenberger that made an emergency landing in the Hudson River in 2009? It was the good ship *Yogi Berra* that arrived first to rescue the passengers huddled on the plane's wings.)

On that special day in '99, both the New York and New Jersey authorities changed the usual route the ferry took, which was to let the riders off in midtown Manhattan by the USS *Intrepid* museum. To get it to Yankee Stadium, they rerouted it all the way around the southern tip of Manhattan island, up the East River, and finally to the Harlem River. It took an hour, but it was a breathtaking ride. Dad may not have moved mountains, but he moved a ferry line. From the pier near the stadium, Dad and Mom were driven to the park and then across the outfield into the infield in a '57 Thunderbird, getting out at home plate for the ceremony. Times do change. In '59, they rode to home plate in a station wagon.

Joe Torre was tickled to death that he was managing the Yankees when Yogi came back home. Had Dad not stayed away so long, he said, "every day would have been Yogi Berra Day. Yogi is a major part of what this team is about." Donnie Mattingly agreed. Even when Dad was in exile, Donnie said, "He was always a Yankee." Humble as Dad was, he told reporters that, rather than seeing his plaque, the youngest members of the Berra clan were more excited being able to do something else. "I've got five granddaughters," he said, "and they all want to meet Derek Jeter."

His fellow surviving Yankees were there for the homecoming. Phil Rizzuto said a few amusing words about his longtime goombah. Whitey, his hair glistening in the sun, stood alongside Bobby Richardson, Dr. Bobby Brown, Don Larsen, Gil McDougald, Joe Pepitone, and many others Dad considered brothers and sons. The saddest thing for Dad was that Joe D and Mickey couldn't be standing there, too, but he knew they were looking down and cheering like everyone else. The Yankees gave him a trip to Italy and would try to arrange for a visit with the pope, so that Dad could reprise his famous greeting, "Hello, Pope."

Dad looked a little overwhelmed by it, fighting to keep his emotions in check. Larsen, appropriately, threw out the first pitch—to the same man he had thrown every pitch of his perfect game in '56. Dad, who borrowed Joe Girardi's mitt—the actual glove he had used for the game was in the Hall of Fame—caught the pitch and, born showman that he was, jogged out to Larsen, a little slower than the last time, and re-created the immortal leap, though he didn't quite get high enough to make it into Don's arms.

Don't tell me somebody up there didn't love Lawrence Peter Berra. David Cone pitched that day, against the Montreal Expos, and the air in the stadium turned from festive to tension-filled as he just kept blowing through the order. A no-hitter doesn't really become a real thing until the sixth, seventh inning. That's generally when the crowd realizes something special is happening. And when Cone got through them, he'd retired every hitter to face him. Amazingly, on the day Dad and Larsen commemorated the biggest highlight of their careers, Cone was pitching a perfect game! Later, Cone said some "magic" had been transferred to him by shaking hands with them just before he took the mound.

Cone came into the ninth leading, three straight outs away from immortality. Even Dad was biting his nails. Back in '56, he was so focused on calling the pitches for Larsen that he didn't feel the electricity in the air; it was all business—until that last strike on my namesake, Dale Mitchell. Today, as a fan, he edged forward in his seat, trying to transfer his iron will to David Cone's arm. Mom, next to him, looked like she was praying. Coney struck out the first batter on three killer sliders, a pitch that when it's working is the most difficult one to hit. The second hitter blooped one to short left that Ricky Ledee appeared to lose in the sun for a moment but then sprinted in and made a wobbly catch. Two down, one to go. Only Orlando Cabrera stood between Cone and Fate. On a 1-1 pitch, Cabrera popped it foul behind third. Scott Brosius roamed under it and put it away. As the stadium burst into a deafening roar, Dad stood and cheered. On the field, Joe Girardi channeled him, grabbing Cone in a bear hug, saying later, "I didn't want to let go." Dad knew exactly how he felt.

Coney was given a ride off the field on the shoulders of his teammates, the third Yankee hurler to throw a perfect game—the second, the portly David Wells, who threw his the year before, was now with the Toronto Blue Jays and called to congratulate the other David in the clubhouse. Don't think it was divine intervention? Well, as it turns out, when Joe Torre was sixteen, he had begged a ticket to that game 5 in '56 and watched from the bleachers when Larsen pitched his historic perfect game. And Cone's came on Joe's fifty-ninth birthday. Sometimes, the Yankee mystique can seem almost scary.

Actually, that was more than a perfect game; it was a perfect day. And Dad was in the middle of it, just like old times, when he was instrumental to almost every big Yankee win. To put it in an even grander perspective, that day came during the last year of a millennium in which Yogi Berra did a whole lot to define the team of that millennium. In a much simpler context, what many folks were happiest about that day was one thing— Yogi was back. The world was good again.

CHAPTER 10

Last of the Ninth

DAD'S GRANDCHILDREN WERE obviously taken with the love and affection all around him on Yogi Berra Day. Larry's daughter, Lindsay, who had just graduated from the University of North Carolina with a degree in communications, earned a job with the Yes Network, the pioneering cable operation the Yankees owned that broadcast all their games, deriving another huge revenue stream for George Steinbrenner. All the kids were talented and athletic, smart and ambitious. Which was why it hurt me that my beautiful daughter Whitney stalled along her own path, having developed a drug problem herself, like me, sliding into the clutches of alcohol and drugs.

I never asked how or why. Because I'd been there, done that, and knew that even the best people succumb to easy gratification. It's funny—and sad—how life repeats when we get older. Because I found myself in the same exact position I had put Dad in, and now I had to be the one to worry myself sick about my own child, support her, and also give some tough love at times. But I needed some assurance myself, that, like my use, hers had nothing to do with any resentment or anger about her family, whether she blamed me for the divorce, whether my habits had anything to do with hers, whether it could have even been genetic.

WHITNEY: I never believed that. I don't think Dad realized how much I learned from him and my grandfather. They were very similar in a lot of ways. Neither of them were smothering. They didn't say much. When I got a little older, every time Dad came by he'd ask coyly who am I dating, what are these guys like? You know, fishing for information because he wanted to protect me. That was funny to me, but I loved him. And Grammy and Grandpa took an interest because they'd had three boys, but most of the grandchildren were girls—seven of the eleven.

But every child has a point where they break free, do things for their own reasons. That's what happened with me when I started using cocaine. Trust me, you don't want to know the details, and that's not what's important. But I started pretty young. I did well in school, played sports, was popular and all that stuff, but I was pretty rebellious and just partied a lot. Cocaine and alcohol were part of it. And it worked for a while, and then it didn't, and it all came to a head around the time when I first went away to college.

You could draw a parallel with Dad. I didn't know the whole story, but from what he's told me, it happened the same way for him, only with him it went on much longer. And I think the reason it didn't for me was that he was a huge piece of my life through all of this, and he'd been through the same thing. I had him for support. He could tell what I was doing. No one knows a coke user like someone who is or was a coke user. In fact, he started to have conversations with me long before I thought that there was any issue. In high school he would start to have conversations, sit me down and talk about things, and I just didn't see it as a problem yet.

My dad and I both have addictive personalities. But I also think that our experiences were different. He was able to manage his life to an extent, and that wasn't my experience. I couldn't pull off "normal." I had that allergy, that gene, where if I put a substance in my body I react differently, and I can't handle it, really. So he knew I was in trouble. He didn't get mad. He was understanding. And from his own experience, he was someone who I trusted and could relate to, listen to. He took me to my first AA meeting when I was like nineteen. But he put it to me the same way his family did to him. It was like, "You're either going to do the right thing and get things together, or we're not in your life and you're on your own." It wasn't like I could go on with what I was doing and be accepted as a Berra.

Like him, that was what I needed to hear. So I did rehab. I went to live in a halfway house in Florida, got a degree in social work from Florida Atlantic University. I worked in substance abuse for a time and found my path in life, to connect with and help other people that are struggling in any way. I work in alternative health and healing. I'm a yoga teacher. I work with reiki, which is an energy exchange healing method. I'm currently in Chinese medicine school, studying healing methods like acupuncture. Thankfully, my problem was over a short period of time, and I have Dad to thank for that. If he ever worried that what I did was somehow his fault, I can say flat out it wasn't. Sometimes it isn't that complicated. You can love someone and still hurt them. But if they love you, the hurt is a way of leading you back to them.

Whitney shaped my life, too. I knew I had to be clean and sober in her eyes. I knew exactly what she was going through and could help her. Naturally, it was difficult at times. I knew all about denial, self-delusion, resistance to good advice, being selfish. But you never falter, never give up. Dad never gave up on me. Your words get through, then get through some more. And, today, at thirty, her life now is all about yoga, healing, and spirituality. We give to each other, the way a father-child relationship should work.

The relationship has made me a better person. I never intended to be an example to others, but as time went on, I was something like a role model. I'd be playing a round at Montclair Golf Club and, knowing who I was and my checkered history, a guy would come up to me and tell me his son came home from college and was addicted to some drug or another. He'd ask me for advice because he couldn't get through to the kid and it was killing him. I'd try to make him see that his son wasn't shaming him—he didn't want to be on drugs—and tell him to hang in there with him, be tough but understanding; tell him the things in the world he needs to care about are things he already has, his family, his life. Tell him he has to make a choice.

There's no foolproof way to take someone off drugs. Sometimes you'll fail; sometimes it will go tragically bad. But like Whitney says, pain can lead to relief and happiness. You don't make yourself the victim of a loved one's problem. It's about something much bigger than that. Dad never once played the victim. In the end, he didn't care about me shaming his name, but the terrifying possibility of losing his son, and me losing my family. When he had to get tough with me, he put it in my hands, and I put it in Whitney's—it's time to choose one of two roads, and you have one last chance to choose the right one. We both chose right. Because we had help from people we loved.

Yogi Berra entered the new millennium as a legitimate elder statesman, a man of great pride, who took his legacy seriously and wouldn't allow anyone to mess with it. In 2003, a one-man play, *Nobody Don't Like Yogi,* came to Broadway with Ben Gazzara playing Dad looking back on his life. Ben had met with Dad at the museum, because Dad loved great actors. However, he never gave his authorization for the project, and after it opened, friends of his who saw it said it had taken liberties with the truth in its portrayal of him, and Mom and Dad refused to see it and lend any credence to a lie.

The real problem with preserving the legacy of Yogi Berra, however, was that Dad himself was too trusting with people who told him how much his name, his brand, was worth. Dad didn't know that he was worth the same as Mickey Mantle and Stan Musial. A guy would come over to the house and say, "I'll give you ten thousand dollars if you sign a couple hundred balls." He'd say, "Okay." He didn't think about what he was getting per baseball. If guys were charging $100 for a signature, they'd get $20,000, double what they gave him. He wasn't getting his market value, and he didn't know any better. He had no clue that his autograph on a baseball brought in a top price.

It wasn't that he didn't have good business judgment. As I say, he never really made a bad investment, never had to worry about money. When my brothers and I had all moved out of the house, and he didn't need all that room anymore, he sold it for a handsome profit, and he and Mom bought a smaller one, a sort of love nest for them in their old age. So he had a golden touch. It was that none of the guys he played with had a head for standing up for themselves when it came to self-worth. They came from a whole different time; jocks then weren't supposed to have any say about what they were worth. They were conditioned that way. And with Dad, he just didn't want to believe anyone was taking advantage of them. He loved the Yankees' owners, loved the GMs. He had trusted Ralph Houk and George Steinbrenner, both of whom stabbed him in the back. Because his philosophy was, anybody that's trying to help you, be nice to them.

His perspective was that of a poor kid from the Hill, who worked his way up and had a beautiful wife and loving kids who grew up in a beautiful home. He had everything he needed, money in the bank, and it was the result of hard work and good values. But that didn't mean we were going to let people rip off his name. After all, his name always meant money for someone, judging by all the commercials he did long after his playing days. All anyone had to do was see his mug on TV and smile, and they'd remember the product. And sponsors were paying all kinds of money to get him in a studio for a few hours. Back in the '50s, a guy from an ad agency would come in the clubhouse and hand him a hundred bucks to do a Marlboro commercial. Now, just one signature on a baseball from his playing days could bring in many times that.

So Timmy and I said, hey let's take this over, because Dad's been getting cheated for so many years. We shut off anyone else claiming to represent him. With Larry, we formed a company in 1994 called LTD, our first initials. Timmy is an expert in the memorabilia field and collection industry and I had the ability to communicate with people. We began to handle all of his licensing. Over the last twenty-five years, anyone wanting to make a deal for signed memorabilia has had to go through LTD. Everything like that is consolidated within the family business, which is the way it should be. I remember when they used to sing "We Are Family" in Pittsburgh. Well, that family lasted one year. We'll be a family forever.

Dad was happy about it. That was how he was introduced to the business of being Yogi late in life, when the stars of the past were suddenly getting big money for card shows and appearances. It wasn't enough for a lot of them. I thought it was demeaning to Mickey and Willie Mays to be paid for greeting people who came into casinos, because they needed money. They weren't being celebrated; they were used as props. Dad would have rather slept on a park bench than do that, and they would get in trouble with baseball for having an association with gambling and had to quit doing it. It was an insult to their greatness and dignity. And that was never going to happen to Yogi Berra.

We saved him a fortune, which was the least I could do to honor the man who gave me so much. With everything controlled to make sure he was rewarded properly, I'm proud to say that only Yogi Berra, among all of the stars of his era, really achieved earning his market value in his lifetime. In fact, he might have had the highest market value of any ballplayer who ever lived. And he deserved every penny. He did so many commercials where he didn't even know what the product was or the name of the company. After he filmed one for Aflac insurance—you might remember him in it, sitting in a barber shop, dispensing Yogi-isms to the befuddled barber and the Aflac duck—someone asked him who it was for. "Amtrak," he said. Same old Yogi. Another, for Visa, co-starred his physical opposite, Yao Ming, the seven-foot-six center for the Houston Rockets at the time. The spot, a classic, had them each responding to a store clerk who keeps saying "Yo!" Ming repeating "Yao!" Dad's line was "gi...Yo-giii." It's only funny if you see and hear it, how he looked into the camera as he patiently repeated, "Yo-giii."

He also had numerous requests to be a keynote speaker or to appear at a banquet. For some, like the Italian American Club, he'd do it for nothing. He received a doctorate of letters from

Washington University in St. Louis and was inducted into the New Jersey Hall of Fame with the actor Jack Nicholson. He gave commencement speeches, many of which were written for him by Mom or Dave Kaplan. It almost seemed as if Dad was in the prime of his life. You couldn't keep up with him. But then, that was an old story.

At the same time that I was putting a lot of work into maintaining his legend and market value, I was putting a lot of work into my own value—to myself. Doing that out of the glare of the public spotlight made life more real, more meaningful than the constant intrusions when you're a pro athlete. I lived quietly, humbly. And I found the woman I'd been waiting for all my life. Her name is Jane Woodruff, a Montclair girl, thirteen years younger than me—imagine that. I'd been divorced fifteen years, living clean, preparing for the next journey. I was ready for love and marriage again, and Jane was sent from heaven.

Jane is a lot more sophisticated than me, that's for sure. She was born and raised in Montclair. However, Jane's mother is from Switzerland. Having a European background, Jane has taught me a lot about how to carry and present myself, which I definitely needed. I'd spent literally half my life in locker rooms, screaming, bumping into people, walking around in my underwear. I'd be in a restaurant, see someone I knew, and yell across the room, completely oblivious to disturbing anyone else. She made me more aware of my personal space and taught me to be cognizant of my surroundings. It was like taking a course from Miss Manners.

Mom and Dad loved Jane, because they knew she was good for me. She is smart, athletic, family-oriented, and extremely cultured. Dad loved that she is also humble. He would always get that look in his eye when he was around people who boasted and talked too much, and she didn't. I definitely married up, which of course is what Dad always said about himself. I knew what he meant. We got married in her Protestant church on May 1, 2004, because I was sort of a lapsed Catholic, and I deferred to Jane, who has strong religious beliefs. Mom and Dad's gift to us was a trip to Rome and Ireland. No, I didn't make it to the Vatican to say, "Hello, Pope." We went on our own up the Amalfi Coast on the Salerno Gulf and stayed on the Isle of Capri off the Sorrentine Peninsula. That was also walking in Dad's footsteps, repeating his journey to the Old Country after D-Day. He knew how beautiful and inspiring it was, and that I would benefit from that experience. He was right. It was two weeks in paradise. Thanks, Mom and Dad.

Dad, meanwhile, was becoming an icon to another generation. He was in constant demand as baseball's prime elder statesman. It didn't matter whether you loved or hated the Yankees. You loved Yogi. In 1999, baseball honored its All-Century Team at Fenway Park in Boston. Dad and Johnny Bench were the catchers. And after the ceremonies, when he was cheered, he walked from the field entrance through the crowd and up into the press box. As he walked up the steps through the stands, every row got up one after the other and stood up for him and clapped for him. That said it all. No old team rivalry could ever eclipse how all baseball fans felt about him.

That of course was a common scene at his "home" park. Dad enjoyed going to Yankee Stadium just to meet with the players and the manager, for the camaraderie. That was in his blood, as it is with all of us who played. He made a ritual of going each spring to Tampa, George's hometown, where the Yankees moved their spring training base in 1995. There, he could don the pinstripes and help the Yankee catchers get their game down. Yet he had no interest in watching games. He'd go to the stadium at three in the afternoon and be home by five. He was nearing his nineties, but with his spry little baby steps and grace, it seemed he would live forever. I believe he wanted to do just that.

He found himself outliving nearly all of his contemporaries and best friends. John McMullen died in 2005; Phil Rizzuto in 2007. Dad had watched Scooter suffer with cancer of the esophagus. After Phil needed an operation that removed half of his stomach, he was put in a nursing home in West Orange, New Jersey, and Dad visited him often, coming away shaken as Phil wasted away. The deaths of John and Scooter hit him hard; sitting in the church for their funerals, then watching them be buried, he had to confront his own mortality, but he never lost that sense of vitality, his love for life. He wanted to enjoy every minute of it.

There would be more losses. George Steinbrenner died in 2010, which saddened him, as he'd established a pretty good relationship with George. And Larry Doby left us in 2003, two years after his beloved wife, Helyn, had died, both of cancer. As he had with John and Phil, Dad had visited both of them during their painful last months, and he was in the congregation for both of their funerals. Knowing the end was near for his friend, he established the Larry Doby Wing at the museum, honoring not only Larry but all the great Negro League players. He wanted Larry to know he would be remembered.

The museum became a wonderfully successful attraction; chartered buses would roll up all the time with either school field trips or seniors who had grown old with him but never forgotten their memories of youth rooting for him. But no good deed goes unpunished, I guess. In 2014, some guys broke into the museum and stole dad's World Series rings, fourteen in all, ten championships and four consolations. It was like a *Mission: Impossible* episode. They actually lowered themselves down from the ceiling on ropes with a lever system and had special jacks. They used glass cutters that opened up the cases like a hot knife through butter. They avoided the laser security sensors, took the rings, and left.

LARRY: They planned it down to the second. It's a five-minute response time for the police to get to the building once the alarms go off. They were in the building for four minutes. They only took Dad's stuff. In the case right next to the rings was Don Larsen's perfect game uniform worth a million dollars, but they didn't take it. There was a Lou Gehrig ball; they didn't take it. They just took Dad's rings and two Hall of Fame plaques. That was it, nothing else.

When we found out, Timmy, Larry, and I talked to him about the theft. He said, "I'm more upset for you guys. I lived it. It's all up here," pointing to his head. "I don't need those rings for the memories. They were for you guys."

Imagine being that unselfish. Sure, he had so many rings that they all seemed to fudge together. But, back then, the ring was a good part of their income. Hank Bauer used to say, "Don't fuck with my ring," another way of saying, "Don't mess with my money." I was more like Dad. My one ring, for the Pirates' '79 championship, was also stolen, years before that. How's that for a terrible coincidence? I had a facsimile ring made for me, because having earned a ring was important to me.

Even so, I was far more concerned with Dad's rings and getting them back. The FBI got involved, but they came up empty. We paid investigators, and we figure the rings are in Russia somewhere, in somebody's safe. You can't really fence them, because no one would want to be known having them. You can't take the chance of someone saying, "Hey, I just saw Yogi Berra's rings." You can't sell them and can't show them to anybody, so why even take them? The FBI says they'll probably turn up because there will be a one-time fence, some secret exchange. They'll try to do it anonymously, and the guy who stole them will get away with it, but at least we'll get the rings back. We're hoping. But I'll tell the robbers a little secret. Some of the rings were replicas, not originals. So when you try to sell them, guys, be prepared for a shock. You won't get what you think.

In his last decade, it seemed Dad was drinking in high honors all the time, some owed him for too long. One of the proudest days of all came in 2009 when the US Navy Memorial honored him with the Lone Sailor Award, which is given each year to a navy veteran who achieved lofty status by applying the touchstones of his service: honor, courage, and commitment. The award was sometimes given to an athlete, such as Stan Musial in 2007 and Arnold Palmer in 2008. It's presented in Washington, DC, and Dad was no stranger there. He had met every president from Truman to Obama and been invited to the White House ten times for state dinners and various functions. He and Mom were greeted warmly by the Obamas that day. Mom said Michelle Obama was stunning. Democrat or Republican, Mom knew what class was. And she still wore her own class and sophistication extraordinarily well.

The only thing that makes me sad about it was that he didn't get his Medal of Freedom, the highest honor an American can receive, while he was still living. They had ninety years to do that. I suppose they thought he'd live forever. It sure looked like he would. Right up until the last few years, he never seemed to age much. His only concession to Father Time were the glasses he'd worn since the '70s. He walked the same, with those graceful little steps, and played golf almost every day in good weather until his knee began to bother him. He and Mom were greeters at the Bob Hope Classic and other big tournaments. He hosted his own tournament, the Yogi Berra Classic in Montclair. The celebrities still loved to be around him. And he loved being anywhere.

When he went to Yankee Stadium for opening day in 2003, he was sitting with Whitey when on the scoreboard were listed the names of Yankees who had died during the off-season. "Boy," he told Whitey, "I hope I never see my name up there."

But age was finally starting to catch up to his body. He

would deal with his knee pain by having cortisone shots and getting the knee joint drained. However, in 2000, unable to walk the golf course properly, he decided to undergo a knee replacement. That surgery is a common procedure for seniors. But as a result, Dad lost his gait. He began to lose muscle definition in his lower body, and his ankles became bloated. Dad had the legs of a football player; his massive thighs were like tree stumps and his calves like big melons. All that muscle tapered to skinny ankles, like a racehorse. But all the swelling made him look different, even though he attacked his rehab and worked out every day. He had made it a ritual every morning to work out with John McMullen at the New Jersey Devils' training facility up until John got sick. But his muscle tone atrophied.

Physically, it wasn't the same Yogi. But he had that old spunk. He wouldn't let pain or weakness stop him from living his life as he wanted. He still got on the plane and went to Tampa for spring training with the Yankees. He and Mom went out for dinner, to the museum, to the golf club. He still played gin with his friends. He was still Yogi, just slower. But the telltale signs of his frustration became more frequent. He couldn't swing a golf club as hard, because, like swinging a baseball bat, the legs generate the power. He'd take a short swing, get the ball halfway down the fairway probably a hundred yards fewer than he used to. Then he would sit in the cart, wincing in pain. He would never complain or make excuses. "I'm getting older. I could hit a baseball farther than I can a golf ball" was his explanation for a lesser quality of life, saying it with a shrug and a little sardonic grin. Not that it sucked getting older, just that he was getting older. But he saw the positives. "Hey, I can get out there and take a swing. I don't care how far it goes," he would say, I imagine that was something like what he must have told Casey Stengel more than a few times, except that when he swung at a ball in his prime, it went out like a missile.

I didn't feel too bad for him—he still beat the pants off me and my brothers when we played cards or Monopoly with him. He still could have sunk more hoops on the driveway sitting on a chair than we could have on two good legs. But when I did see him in obvious discomfort, I wished that he'd never had the knee replacement. He would have been better off living with the pain by continuing the shots and draining his knee. Because with all the bloating in his legs, he lost more mobility and then could barely walk at all at times; when he tried, he would sometimes fall down.

That was shocking to us. This was Yogi Berra. A man as graceful as any man could be, yet a man we now had to worry might fall and break a hip or an ankle. One time, he went out to get a haircut, and while walking out of the house he fell down the stairs outside. He was okay but had nasty cuts on his forehead, nose, and arms. As proud as he was, he waved off any help. He didn't go in the house and clean himself off. He struggled to his feet, slid into the driver's seat of his car, and drove to the barbershop. He walked in there a bloody mess. But he got his haircut. He always finished what he started.

A couple of times when he fell, we had to bring him to the hospital because we didn't know if he had a concussion. And he hated hospitals. Hated 'em. But he would be spending some time there. After a while, he developed an irregular heartbeat and went in for tests. The doctors once tried to shock his heart back to its regular pace, but it didn't work, so he started taking

Coumadin to prevent a stroke or heart attack. And being on this kind of regimen had an effect on his personality. He became withdrawn and a little closed off. Taking the pills made him feel cold, so he bundled up inside the house and stopped wanting to go out and do the things he loved doing.

Mentally, he was still sharp as a tack. On good days, he was spry and in a good mood, telling his jokes. He was also more immersed in protecting his legacy than he had been before. In 2014, for example, he and Mom gave their blessing to another play that focused on their life together, *Bronx Bombers*. It was produced by the same people who had staged *Lombardi* and *Magic/Bird*, and they made sure to obtain the approval of baseball, the Yankees, and Mom and Dad, who revealed a lot about themselves, before putting it on Broadway. In the show, Yogi dreams about interacting with Yankee stars past and present, and his relationship with Mom is, accurately, the center of his life. The lead roles were played by Peter Scolari and his wife, Tracy Shayne, who didn't need to act to show love and affection for each other. I enjoyed it, but it's just so hard for an actor to nail what Dad was really like; many have tried, such as Paul Borghese in Billy Crystal's 2001 HBO movie *61**, but none have gotten it right.

With Yogi Berra, you had to be there. You had to experience the quirks to know that whatever he said, he never wanted to hurt anyone. You had to hear him when he ran into an old acquaintance and growled, "Hey, what the hell are you doin' here?" to know that while he sounded gruff and grumbly, it was just his way of joshing you, putting you at ease. He wasn't dour or distant; he was just Yogi being Yogi. Lord knows, he did that with us all the time, and we loved it when he did. Because that was the essence of the man I grew up with, and I gave thanks to God for keeping him around as long as he did.

The same could be said for my mom. In 2010, Carmen Short Berra was eighty-five years old and seemed ageless. She was in good health and as beautiful and regal as a queen. She and Dad celebrated their sixty-fifth anniversary on January 26 at the museum, where they loved to spend time saying hello to the tourists who came through. Mom had dealt with small things that cropped up with regard to her health, but she was notorious for ignoring anything wrong with her. She didn't want anybody to know if there was something going on. She had her own doctor, kept to herself. I had no idea that she also had an irregular heartbeat and was on Coumadin; she never told us. One day, on her way back to her car from a coffee shop, she heard what sounded like a click inside her head, and then everything was spinning, and she was seeing things upside down.

She sat down on the curb, managed to get out her cell phone, and felt the buttons to call 911. An ambulance came, picked her up from the curb, and took her to the hospital. The doctors said she'd had a sudden aneurysm, a small amount of bleeding in her brain, and that it caused a small stroke. When they called my brothers and me, we went and picked up Dad and raced to the hospital. When we got there, she was in a room and complained of a headache along with a very weird feeling of being separated from her body and everyone sounding like they were speaking to her from an echo chamber. Leave it to her, after a week in the hospital, where we all stayed with her 'round the clock, she made enough of a recovery to go home. Larry, who had recently gotten divorced, moved in with them and could help both Mom and Dad move around.

They were still together and happy about that. However, that interim didn't last long. Mom and Dad were functional but needed a lot of help because neither one could go up the stairs unassisted. We hired care workers to take care of our parents, who needed to be monitored around the clock. Dad was still falling down, and we lived in fear that he'd fall down the stairs and have a catastrophic accident. For his own safety, we convinced him to move into the best assisted living place we could find, Crane's Mill, in West Caldwell, around twenty minutes from the house. It was a huge decision for him to be taken from his house, his castle. But he didn't fight it. The day he left, we all cried, but Dad was, well, Yogi.

"I'll be back," he said, a vow we knew he would not be able to keep.

Mom stayed a little longer at home, with a full-time caretaker. She was taken for visits to Dad, but she was deteriorating as well and couldn't bear being separated from the man she loved. She missed him so much that she said she wanted to be with him. So we moved her to Crane's Mill, too, into a room right next to his. We put a doorway in and made their rooms adjoining. Neither one of them liked it there. They both wanted to be home, but they made the best of it.

Then Mom had another stroke and things went bad fast. She lost her ability to swallow. She could only swallow if they made her food and water into a gel so she could get it down her throat with a straw. Her quality of life was reduced to the point where she didn't want to go on.

It got so hard for her that she couldn't take it anymore. She told the doctors and attendants that she wanted to stop all that and let her life end. When we were visiting her one day, she said, "I'm going to refuse medication, and I'm not going to eat. I'm not going to live like this." We tried to convince her otherwise, though there was nothing anyone could do to make her life better. It's beyond heartbreaking when you know your parent is in pain, but the trade-off for ending the pain was to end her life. The moral and ethical issues involved in that kind of a decision pale before the simple, gut-wrenching reality that this is your mother, the person who brought you into the world, and that when she goes, much of your own life will go with her. So we tried to keep her alive.

"Mom, you can get better," we'd say. But she'd say, "No, this is what I want to do." Which was to die with the same dignity with which she lived.

Dad couldn't do anything for her; he was declining fast, too, his organs failing. He had congestive heart failure, water was filling his lungs and joints, his heart was not working hard enough to drain the fluid. He couldn't walk, and he could barely shake your hand because he was weak and his fingers were blown up like little balloons. He had no interest in watching TV anymore; he just sat kind of slumped over, staring. It was all I could do to keep from crying, which I knew he wouldn't want to see. I kept it upbeat, but I was dying inside, too.

We hired additional hospice workers to help Mom, and they got her to eat a little. But in the early spring, the time of year that used to be so exciting to both of them and to each of us, all she could really do was read. She constantly read books, basically waiting to die. The people at the facility and the hospice people said, "If that's what she wants, there's nothing we can do."

On March 5, 2014, I got a call that I better get there quickly. The whole family gathered around her. She was weak and couldn't get out of bed. We all knew this might be her last day. Larry, Timmy, and I went and got Dad from physical therapy. We brought him to Mom's bedside. And then, in a sight I will never forget, out of nowhere, Yogi Berra became young again, if just for a minute. Drawing up all his inner strength, he suddenly stood up out of his wheelchair, with vigor, unaided, as if some hidden force was pulling him up. His voice, which had gotten so weak and faint, was strong again, as it was over sixty-five years ago when he asked her out on their first date. Looking straight at Mom, in perfect Yogi Berra pitch, he made his last wish.

"Come on, Carm," he told her. "Let's get the hell out of here. Let's go back home. You're all right. We'll have a drink together. C'mon, Larry, Timmy, and Dale are here. Let's all go home." Mom managed to put on a little smile, almost a smirk, as if it came from her past, too. "Sure, Yogi," she said.

It was all she needed to say. Because at that moment, both of them were transported back in time, to when they were lovesick kids on the Hill. Some might say it was a miracle. I say it was their love that broke through the reality of sickness and pain, giving them one last minute to share before death would they part.

We were all there until late at night before going home. Mom's good friend Joni Bronander stayed with her along with Larry's daughter Maria. As they were sitting at her bedside, they saw Mom's head rise from the bed and her arms reached for the sky, as if she saw a light or something. She gently lowered herself back into the bed and passed.

She was still beautiful, still regal. Lying on her white bed sheets, she seemed gossamerlike, forever the queen. When the producers of *Bronx Bombers* were casting the show, they specified that the character of Carmen Berra had to be "the epitome of all that a Yankee wife should be. She exudes confidence without ever seeming pompous, and exemplifies the good citizen without ever appearing plain. She is dynamic, energetic, embodies sex appeal; men are attracted to her and women are drawn to her. A fashion maven, she has an instinct for saying, doing, and wearing the right things at all the right times. All respect and admire her." Dad said all that and more, in his eyes, whenever he looked at her.

We held her funeral at Immaculate Conception Church in Montclair, where we had worshiped for fifty years, and laid her to rest in Gates of Heaven cemetery. Dad was there, and we made sure to spend the rest of the day with him at Crane's Mill. But it was an unspoken thought for many of us that we would be retracing these same steps soon for Dad.

We always knew he wouldn't live long if Mom went first. They were a big part of each other, 'til death did they part. Dad didn't speak much about her, but she was on his mind. He was still capable of having a very brief conversation and of being the same old lovably cantankerous Yogi, especially when I tried to ease his mind about coming to the end.

"Dad," I told him, "you're going to go soon, and you're going to go to heaven, and you're going to go join Mom up there."

He glared at me. "What do you mean me—why don't *you* go join Mom?" he rasped. "I don't want to go yet."

Because he loved life and lived every minute of it to the fullest. He never, even while in Crane's, liked to admit he was terminally sick. But he knew he had to face it. A few days before he died, I asked him how he was feeling.

"Something ain't right," he said. "I don't know where the hell I'm at. This ain't good."

He made it through almost nineteen very sad months after Mom died. On September 22—sixty-nine years to the day from his first game as a Yankee—he was doing badly, and the first one the hospital called was Larry.

LARRY: I got the call to come right over, time was running out, and I made it and I was hugging him, saying Mom's coming for you. And Tim also made it to the home just before he passed away. It was amazing how he held on the whole time. The day he died, as weak as he was, he weighed the same as in his playing days, 190 pounds. He didn't lose any weight like most people do when they get older. People used to come in, or the nurses used to come in and help him and everything, and they'd go, Jesus criminy, what the hell is this guy doing, he's like a rock. It wasn't like he was wasting away.

It was like he was hanging on, waiting for the right moment to let go. And the nurse said later that when she heard I'd gotten there, she hugged and told him, "Larry's here, Yogi. You can leave now." And that's when finally, he let go and stopped breathing. I'd watched both my mother and father die. It's not something you ever would have thought you'd see when you were young and they were young. But not even Yogi Berra could live forever.

TIM: I was at Mom and Dad's house when Larry called. I got there just in time. I tried to prepare myself for months, get it in my mind that my father was dying, but he was that kind of a man who always beat the odds. He fooled everyone who counted him out. It was like he had a line to God. But, you know, he had seen enough. With Mom gone, he didn't have that great anchor, his life partner. He was ready to go. And we'd prepared ourselves for that. But you never really can. It still hurts.

I was running up the steps from the parking lot when he died. My brothers were there, each holding one of his hands. I bent over and kissed him on his forehead when I got to him. We prayed over him, and as I did I realized he was as much a friend to me as a father, just as he was to people who never knew him. I was incredibly sad that our family and the world had lost a true original, and I cried having lost our parents—as had Dad—so close together in time. But I wasn't consumed by sadness and grief. Because that was the way Dad had taught me, that life was meant to be enjoyed, that a good life was something to celebrate, not mourn, when it was over. And I just knew he was back with my mom and playing baseball again with his old teammates. He was young again and out of pain. I was, and am, convinced of that.

LARRY: My hero died in front of my eyes. But we had sixty-six years together, and you have a lot of memories of a man who lives that long and that well. He never cheated himself, his family, or his fans, not for a minute. He showed what life is supposed to be like, how it's supposed to be lived. And so I feel like Dale. I remember him for all the good memories. I try to laugh, not cry.

TIM: Your first thought is, my dad won't be there any-more; there's a big hole now in my life. But there are a million things that came to mind about him. That's his legacy more than anything he did on a baseball field. He packed a lot of living into ninety years. No one ever lived a fuller, better life than my dad.

He had given ninety glorious years to baseball and humanity. He had absolutely no complaints. He'd lived his dream, mar-ried his queen, raised a family he loved. For us, he was all any child could ever ask for in a father, and that's something you carry with you always, until you die. Even if you didn't know him, you thought you did. You don't have to idealize a man like Yogi Berra; he was perfect just how he was. For me, I had to live with the guilt of causing him pain, but also the satisfac-tion that he knew I had learned what he had tried to drum into me at a young age. It took too long, but as he said of those long

shadows that used to engulf Yankee Stadium on those magical fall afternoons, it gets late early. I guess that's another way
of saying better late than never. Dad always said he wouldn't
change a thing in his life. He knew he didn't ever have to.

**LARRY: We wanted Dale to do the eulogy. He'd had
to find out what Dad meant to him the hard way. He's
caused Dad the most worry and we knew he wanted to
say thank you in public, for the world to hear.**

When he died, the *New York Times* headline was: YOGI
BERRA, YANKEE WHO BUILT HIS STARDOM 90 PERCENT ON SKILL
AND HALF ON WIT, DIES AT 90. The article called him "one of
baseball's greatest catchers and characters." That was the tone
of his funeral, which was fit for a president or king. The service
was carried live on local TV from the Church of the Immaculate Conception. It was standing room only, all four hundred
seats taken, the building roped off so that his fans could stand
outside and listen to the service on a public address system. I
gave the eulogy for the family, setting the tone by telling a joke
he would have loved: that when he came to the pearly gates of
heaven, St. Peter wasn't there yet; when he showed up, Dad
greeted him with "You're late." But, in reality, it was perfect
timing.

Standing a few feet from the table on which Dad's urn sat
next to a miniature bronze catcher's mitt, I spoke about what
he'd meant to me, to us, to baseball, to America, without ever
trying to be anything but who he was, the redoubtable Mr.
Berra. I was so proud, too, when Whitney rose to lead the

congregation in reading from the Bible. She broke down briefly, and said, "Sorry," though not a soul blamed her. I think it was at that moment that she knew how special it was to be a branch of Yogi Berra's family tree.

Joe Torre then delivered a eulogy for the baseball community, saying Dad "personified the American dream." And Cardinal Timothy Dolan of the Catholic Archdiocese of New York gave another eulogy, equating Dad with another famous son of Italian immigrants, Pope Francis. Both men, he said with a grin, even had similarly oversized ears. Yankees past and present were there, led by Derek Jeter, who told a few amusing anecdotes. Baseball commissioner Rob Manfred was there. Jackie Robinson's beautiful widow, Rachel, was there. Numerous political leaders were there. Hundreds of navy sailors, honoring Dad's service during World War II, ringed the church, as they would if a president had died. A navy trumpeter played "Taps."

My brothers and I walked down the aisle out of the church, a weeping Timmy holding the urn that held our father's ashes. We then formed a long procession to the Gates of Heaven cemetery, led by the longest police motorcycle brigade I've ever seen. Then we buried him next to Mom, together in eternity. We also arranged for a public memorial at the museum the following Sunday. No one had any doubt that Yogi Berra had passed right through those pearly gates on his way to heaven, right on time. On that day, not only New York mourned and paid tribute to him, as well as laughed out loud as people recalled his famous "Yogi-isms," one of which I thought about with a smile: "You should always go to other people's funerals. Otherwise, they won't come to yours."

All of America, all the world, paused for a moment that day to remember what Dad meant to them. They had memories of him that will never fade, and personal feelings about him even if they had never met him. One of the many newspaper reporters who were at the funeral, the *New York Times'* Harvey Araton, who had written a touching book called *Driving Mr. Yogi* about how Ron Guidry used to drive Dad around Tampa during spring training in his later years, told of an elderly woman who had waited outside the chapel for hours. She had never met my father but drove hundreds of miles to be at his funeral. She and dozens of others cried as the service was carried on loudspeakers. When the mourners began to come outside, the woman begged people if she could have one of their programs. When someone gave his to her, she again wept.

"Standing out here," she said, "I felt as if I could see through the bricks, as if I was inside. I've been a Yankees fan since I grew up, but I always believed that Yogi Berra was much more than a ballplayer."

To that, I can only say one thing. Amen.

His popularity never seems to fade. On November 24, 2015, only two months after he left us, Dad was awarded the highest honor a citizen can receive, the Presidential Medal of Freedom, in a ceremony at the White House. Larry accepted it for him, President Obama draping the medal around his neck. The president gave a touching speech, calling him "an American treasure" and relating some of the famous Yogi-isms. There were a lot of laughs, and a lot of tears, on that day.

Meanwhile, way further down on the radar, I reached my sixties, healthy and happy. My family grew. Jane gave birth to two daughters, Alexandra and Kay, making me the proud father of three girls, who all have the Yogi genes. Alexandra is a pretty good little softball player, and Kay a wonderful gymnast. To be able to resume being a husband and father again in my sixties is a gift, as far as I'm concerned.

Larry lived in our parents' house for a while, but we reluctantly sold it. Still, every time we pass it, and especially when we pass the magnificent house we grew up in, we're transported back in time. And we smile. Never have Larry, Tim, or I ever considered for a minute moving out of the Montclair area. We have continued to live right down the street from each other. If you never understood why Jersey boy Bruce Springsteen's song "My Hometown" touches the soul so deeply, you've never lived in a town like Montclair your whole life.

As I write this, Dad's been gone three years, yet I feel as close to him as I ever did. It's common wisdom that you don't know what you had until it's gone. It's still hard to believe he's not around, that I can't call him for advice when I'm feeling low or share when I feel good. My brothers and I talk about him all the time. What he would have said. How he communicated. His funny ways. How he would never embarrass anybody. How he was the most unique man in the world. How completely confident and incredibly secure he was with himself. More than anyone I know, he was unaffected. Completely unaffected. His relationship with the guy who owns the corner store was as important to him as his relationship with a corporate CEO.

He had less of an ego than anyone I've ever known. Near the end, I would sit with him and talk about the old days. I'd ask, "Dad, what was it like in '73 with the Mets? What was it like with those guys?" He'd say, "Good."

"Well, you know," I went on, trying to get a reaction, "Seaver sometimes overlooks you. He talks about Hodges all the time and doesn't even mention you."

"He pitched good for me."

"What was it like when you managed the Yankees?"

"That was good, too."

"What about Mickey and Whitey?"

"They played good for me. And Pepitone. I made him play first base every day and he had a hell of a year."

You just couldn't get a negative word out of him. It's not an exaggeration to say that I never met a player, or anyone else, who didn't love him. And I know why. He loved them, too. If you ever met him, you felt an immediate calm. It was the same thing Jack Maguire—or Bobby Hoffman—felt so long ago when one of them looked at him and saw Buddha. For me, that calm was more effective than a swift kick in the ass, which I really deserved. I still feel his calm thinking of him.

That had a lot to do with me becoming comfortable enough with my past to relive it in these pages. It was definitely painful, but what resonated the most of everything he ever told me was that you don't learn from your hits; you learn from your errors. I am the proof of that. What did I learn? That when you come to a fork in the road, you take it. I took it.

I'm still on that road, still following the Yogi rules. I'm punctual. I'm appropriate. I try to do the right thing all the time. And I know how to play the game of life. If I get stopped by a cop because I was messing with my GPS and switched lanes by accident, he could give me a hard time. But I'll be very respectful, and he'll say, "Ah, go ahead, you're all right." He doesn't ask to see my license, doesn't know my name. Just by my voice inflection, the way I look at him, he knows I'm okay. He knows I'm sober. He knows I'm clean. There's nothing in my voice that sounds like I'm concerned about being stopped. I have that whole thing down pat. Thanks, Dad.

If there's one thing I learned writing this book, it's something he taught us all with one of those Yogi-isms: if the world was perfect, it wouldn't be. Back when youth was being wasted on me as a young man, I wouldn't have had a clue what that meant. Today, I do. Life is not about being perfect; it's about living with not being perfect. I'm still obsessive, still have an addictive personality. But it's all channeled into something positive, although I'm just a bit too addicted to golf. I have a five or six handicap, and I'm out there all the time. And I'm obsessed with it to the point where it affects my marriage and my family. My kids will say, "Dad, watch a movie with me," and I have to beg off, because of golf. I've got to stop doing that. I'm a better father the second time around, but not good enough, not yet.

Then, too, just like Dad, I have to learn how to understand the kids of a new generation. I try. But just try explaining to them what rock-and-roll is, who Eric Clapton is, who Ritchie

Blackmore is, who Ginger Baker is, get them to listen to a guitar riff, a drum solo. I had to learn why Dad liked the Mills Brothers and Gene Krupa, so they can appreciate rock, too, but few of them do. However, the culture that birthed both Yogi Berra and rock-and-roll, as the old song goes, "is here to stay, it will never die."

I also obsess over elevating New Jersey. Rutgers joined the Big 10 a few years ago and they are terrible in sports. The problem is that New Jersey high school sports are really good, and if we just kept our kids home, Rutgers could compete nationally, on the same level as Tennessee, Alabama, USC, and Penn State. But the Jersey kids don't stay home; they go everywhere else and become All-Americans. Or they go to the shore and do tacky reality shows. Well, one day we will rise.

As for baseball, I have good memories of it—and a regret. The regret is not knowing how good I could have been. I may be overstating it, or I may have too high an opinion of my abilities, but I think I could have made a few All-Star teams if not for a few of my poor choices. I don't watch ballgames on TV much, and I never go to the ballpark. I'm not a Mets fan anymore. I put all that out of my mind and my soul. I loved coaching Whitney's softball teams, and I currently help coach Alexandra's softball team. If I had sons, I might be more involved and keep up with big-league opportunities for them, because if I did have boys, they'd probably have the same genes Dad handed down to his boys. As it is, my daughters are talented athletes. Even Jane is a tremendous athlete; she can play any sport, kills at tennis and paddle tennis. Sports are a large part of the Berra family. That's undeniable. It will always be that way. But when I retired, I never wanted to pick up a bat or ball again, or care about the big leagues. That's my past, and it will stay there.

LARRY: Dale's sixty-one now and looks thirty-five. He's amazing. He's still hyper as hell. He's a health freak now. He goes, "What are you eating that for? You're not supposed to eat that. Eat this instead. What are you drinking?" He'll really come after you. I'll go, "Will you be quiet?" But I know he's right.

He means what he says about baseball. We had played together in the early 2000s in a softball league. We played in local tournaments in Jersey. And Dad got a kick out of watching us. He'd rag us, you know: "Ya gotta bend over for a grounder," but he was proud of us getting out there and competing. This is how competitive Dale was; he said, "I'm going to play with you until we win the state tournament." So he played, we won it, and he threw his glove into the trunk of his car and said, "That's it for me." He was like Dad, who never played softball or in Old-Timers' games. He didn't want to be the old Yogi, only the prime Yogi. And he would only do it if he won.

[Dale] didn't take that glove out of the trunk for sixteen years. Then, I convinced him to play again, and he did. It's two guys over sixty playing on a team, laughing, happy to be active. It's great having him back, enjoying his life so much. We don't care about who wins. I can't run because of my knee, but they made that rule to help me out. We just do what we can. We both have had our ups and downs, but one thing we always had in common was that we were Yogi Berra's sons. That was our saving grace.

One of the last things Dad said to me wasn't a Yogi-ism. He said that people who turn their life around get a lot of respect. I'm proud of the fact that I've been sober for the last twenty-seven years, and there's nothing that will prevent me from remaining that way. For him. And for me.

If he were here, he would be asking what he always did whenever he saw me—"You all right, kid?" And that sly smile would creep across his face when I would tell him, "Yeah, Dad, I'm all right." Well, somewhere up where he is, sipping a vodka with Mom and telling old stories with Mickey, he knows that. And between sips, I can almost hear him saying what he always did.

"Kid, that's all I wanna hear."

That will get me through another day.

IMAGE CREDITS

All photographs courtesy of the author, with the following exceptions: photograph of Yogi with his wife, Carmen, and their children on page 3, © Marvin E. Newman; photograph of Yogi and a young Dale arriving at Yankee Stadium on page 3, NY Daily News Archive via Getty Images; photograph of Dale and Yogi together in Niagara Falls in 1975 on page 4, Associated Press; photograph of Manager Chuck Tanner congratulating Dale on a home run on page 5, Bettmann / Getty Images; photograph of Dale embracing Yogi after joining the Yankees on page 5, B. Bennett / Bruce Bennett Studios / Getty Images; photographs of Dale hitting a game-winning home run for the Yankees and of being congratulated by his Yankees teammates, both on page 6, by Bob Olen, courtesy of the author and the Yogi Berra Museum.